Cambridge Elements

Elements in the Philosophy of Søren Kierkegaard
edited by
Rick Anthony Furtak
Colorado College

KIERKEGAARD, SOCRATES, AND THE MEANING OF LIFE

Rick Anthony Furtak
Colorado College

Shaftesbury Road, Cambridge CB2 8EA, United Kingdom

One Liberty Plaza, 20th Floor, New York, NY 10006, USA

477 Williamstown Road, Port Melbourne, VIC 3207, Australia

314–321, 3rd Floor, Plot 3, Splendor Forum, Jasola District Centre, New Delhi – 110025, India

103 Penang Road, #05–06/07, Visioncrest Commercial, Singapore 238467

Cambridge University Press is part of Cambridge University Press & Assessment, a department of the University of Cambridge.

We share the University's mission to contribute to society through the pursuit of education, learning and research at the highest international levels of excellence.

www.cambridge.org
Information on this title: www.cambridge.org/9781009616089

DOI: 10.1017/9781009616072

© Rick Anthony Furtak 2025

This publication is in copyright. Subject to statutory exception and to the provisions of relevant collective licensing agreements, no reproduction of any part may take place without the written permission of Cambridge University Press & Assessment.

When citing this work, please include a reference to the DOI 10.1017/9781009616072

First published 2025

A catalogue record for this publication is available from the British Library

ISBN 978-1-009-61608-9 Hardback
ISBN 978-1-009-61609-6 Paperback
ISSN 3033-4977 (online)
ISSN 3033-4969 (print)

Cambridge University Press & Assessment has no responsibility for the persistence or accuracy of URLs for external or third-party internet websites referred to in this publication and does not guarantee that any content on such websites is, or will remain, accurate or appropriate.

For EU product safety concerns, contact us at Calle de José Abascal, 56, 1°, 28003 Madrid, Spain, or email eugpsr@cambridge.org.

Kierkegaard, Socrates, and the Meaning of Life

Elements in the Philosophy of Søren Kierkegaard

DOI: 10.1017/9781009616072
First published online: March 2025

Rick Anthony Furtak
Colorado College

Author for correspondence: Rick Anthony Furtak, rfurtak@coloradocollege.edu

Abstract: Kierkegaard's lifelong fascination with the figure of Socrates has many aspects, but prominent among them is his admiration for the way Socrates was devoted to his divinely ordained mission as a philosopher. To have such a destiny, revealed through what one loves and is passionate about as well as through a feeling of vocation, is a necessary condition of leading a meaningful life, according to Kierkegaard. Examining what Kierkegaard has to say about the meaning of life requires looking at his conception of "subjective truth," as well as how he understands the ancient ideal of "amor fati," a notion that Nietzsche would subsequently take up, but that Kierkegaard understands in a manner that is distinctly his own, and that he sought to put into practice in his own existence. Our life is a work of art, but we are not the artist.

Keywords: meaning, truth, socrates, faith, existentialism

© Rick Anthony Furtak 2025

ISBNs: 9781009616089 (HB), 9781009616096 (PB), 9781009616072 (OC)
ISSNs: 3033-4977 (online) 3033-4969 (print)

Contents

1 Socrates and "another side of the truth": Subjectivity and Felt Conviction 1

2 "Religiousness lies in being deeply moved": Love and Passionate Inspiration 23

3 "So powerful an urge ...": Finding the Meaning of *Each* Life 28

4 "The true life of the individual": Kierkegaardian *Amor Fati* 33

References 40

1 Socrates and "another side of the truth": Subjectivity and Felt Conviction

And when the Lord saw that he turned aside to look, God called to him out of the midst of the bush, and He cried, "Moses!" And he said, "Here I am." God said: "Do not come near! Remove thy sandals from thy feet, for the place where you stand is holy ground." Moses hid his face; as he was afraid to look upon God.

— Exodus 3:4–6

Isaiah answer'd: "I saw no God, nor heard any, in a finite organical perception: but my senses discovered the infinite in every thing, and as I was then perswaded [sic], & I remain confirm'd, that the voice of honest indignation is the voice of God. I cared not for consequences, but wrote." Then I asked: "Does a firm perswasion that a thing is so, make it so?" He replied: "All poets believe that it does, & in ages of imagination this firm perswasion removed mountains; but many are not capable of a firm perswasion of any thing."

Improvement makes for strait [sic] roads, but the crooked roads without Improvement are roads of Genius.

— William Blake, *The Marriage of Heaven and Hell*, "A Memorable Fancy"

Human life is poetry. It's we who live it, unconsciously, day by day, . . . yet in its inviolable wholeness it lives us, it composes us. This is something far different from the old cliché, "Turn your life into a work of art"; we are works of art – but we are not the artist.

— Lou Andreas-Salomé, *Looking Back: Memoirs*

For Kierkegaard, a supremely meaningful life requires having a personal destiny formed in relation to God, and remaining faithful to our greatest loves and passions. Since love and God are not two but one, these twin desiderata tend to merge. Kierkegaard's admiration for the spirit of classical Greek philosophy, and particularly for Socrates, cannot be overstated.

Near the very end of his life, Kierkegaard writes that "the only analogy I have before me is Socrates" (KW 23, 341). Socrates was his intellectual hero, so he provides an obvious starting point for this Element. For, when Camus portrays "the fundamental question of philosophy" as whether, and on what terms, life is worth living,[1] he is reviving a Socratic conception of philosophy (Furtak 2013a).

It is frequently observed that some of the early Greek thinkers, from the pre-Socratics through Aristotle, had interests that included naturalistic metaphysics. A contemporary bias in favor of all things scientific can entail an overemphasis on this, and a voluntary ignoring of other overlaps – between, for instance,

---

[1] Camus (1991, 3–4).

2   *The Philosophy of Søren Kierkegaard*

ancient philosophy and poetry, or ancient philosophy and religion. Numerous classical Greek thinkers wrote poetically, Plato included, and very few were atheists. Narrow, modish assumptions about rationality, and about philosophy itself, "persistently distort and misrepresent" the ancient Greek world.[2] It is accurate enough to state that ancient Greek philosophers were dedicated to reason, as long as we keep in mind that their "conception of 'reason' was richer and more complex than our own" (Nightingale 2021, 171).

Here are two examples suggesting that to question traditional views, for the early Greek thinkers, does not require elevating scientific evidence over the literary and the religious as such. The itinerant poet-philosopher Xenophanes, originally of Colophon, is well-known as a critic of deities made in human form: "If cattle or horses or lions had hands and could draw / And could sculpture like men, then the horses would draw their gods / Like horses, and cattle like cattle, and each would then shape / Bodies of gods in the likeness, each kind, of its own."[3] Yet this critique of anthromorphic gods and goddesses such as those found in Homer's polytheistic vision and in the popular imagination serves the purpose of a heterodox theism: there is, Xenophanes asserts, "One God, greatest among gods and human beings, / In no way similar to mortals either in body or in thought."[4] And the poet Sappho of Lesbos, roughly a contemporary of the consensus "first philosopher" Thales, already takes a stand against the frequently war-glorifying Homeric epics when she writes, "Some say an army on horseback, / some say on foot, and some say ships / are the most beautiful things / on this black earth, / but I say / it is whatever you love."[5] She offers an alternate theory of value and anticipates the discussions of love in Plato's *Symposium*.

At a loss to characterize what defines the family resemblance among modern existential philosophers, Walter Kaufmann at one point refers to "their perfervid individualism."[6] This is more of an apt description than it might initially seem to be, and it captures what distinguishes the emergence of early Greek philosophy as well. The ancient philosophers' avid quest to think for themselves allows them to show us the possibilities that we might embrace, for they are never simply a mirror of their context. They offer us alternatives to the most prevalent

---

[2] Kingsley (1995, 372–373).

[3] Fragment 15 (Kirk, Raven, and Schofield 1983, 168–169), trans. by Karl Popper, cited in Magee (2001, 16).

[4] Fragment 23 (Kirk, Raven, and Schofield 1983, 169–170), modified translation. See also Fragments 24–26. Cf. Stephen R. L. Clark (1997).

[5] Poem 31, translated by Stanley Lombardo. On this fragment, see Zellner (2007). See also Elkins (2020).

[6] Kaufmann (1975, 11).

Kierkegaard, Socrates, and the Meaning of Life

vantage points, rescuing us from being intellectually a mere reflex of where and when we happened to be born. They both disprove and liberate us from "the insipid tenet that every thought is the product of its time," inviting us to bear the weight of questions that are always new for each of us,[7] for which there is no answer in the back of the book. And they may help us to discover an interpretation of existence that relates to our deepest perplexities and our highest aspirations.

A criterion of individuality in philosophical vision serves well to distinguish the first Greek philosophers from what came before. For a philosophy could be defined as a framework through which we make sense of the world and our place in it, whether implicitly by virtue of our upbringing or more deliberately through critical evaluation. Many ancient Greeks took for granted the Homeric view of things, which no doubt qualifies as a worldview,[8] and as we shall see, it operates in the background of subsequent philosophizing – not least in Plato's dialogues, which selectively integrate and transform it for their own purposes.[9] Critical evaluation of a given framework is crucial: one is not a philosopher just by virtue of holding opinions, even if the unreflective adherent of the Homeric worldview does in a sense *have* a philosophy.

This is not to say that theoretical inquiry, the questioning and modification of inherited ideas, is more important than upholding an existential attitude: theory without practice is just as bad as practice without a consciously formulated theoretical outlook. Both are essential to the ancient Greeks. Implicitly following Stoic precepts because, say, one grew up male in a macho culture differs from formulating *and* following Stoic doctrine – as Chrysippus did – or critically revising that doctrine and striving to enact one's revised version of Stoic ethics – as Aristo of Chios and Dionysius of Heraclea, for instance, are said to have done.[10]

So we should ask ourselves, even when encountering the more apparently naturalistic arguments found in some pre-Socratic thinkers, what pertinence

---

[7] Sloterdijk (2013, 66). To embrace the insipid tenet, he adds, offers us an easy way to escape the burden of perennial philosophy. Another contemporary author phrases it this way: "It's naïve to think that philosophy can be practiced, and preserved, without some degree of economic and political stability and support. Yet it's cynical to think that philosophy is never anything more than an expression of political and economic power" – Adamson (2014, xii).

[8] See Irwin (1989, 6–17); Harold (2004, 1).

[9] One could argue that Christianity would do the same with aspects of classical Greek thought. Does this make everyone engaged in Christian practice into a philosopher? For an affirmative answer, see Hadot (2002, 237–252). Cf. Hadot (1995, 272): "In ancient philosophy, it was not only Chrysippus or Epicurus who [as theorists] were considered philosophers. Rather, every person who lived according to the precepts of Chrysippus or Epicurus was every bit as much of a philosopher as they." I think this goes a little too far. On Hadot's tendency to elevate practice *over* theory, see Aubry (2013).

[10] On Aristo and Dionysius, see Diogenes Laertius, *Lives* 7.160–164, 7.166–167.

4   *The Philosophy of Søren Kierkegaard*

does this idea have for human beings who seek to understand reality and their role in it? The pursuit of wisdom that relates to human life is such a prominent theme throughout this period that our principle of interpretation ought to be that all theorizing relates to practice, unless there are compelling reasons to conclude otherwise in a concrete instance.[11] This means that we cannot approach the ancient Greeks with the prevalent modern conception of philosophy in mind, which presumes that abstract reflections and theoretical positions are entities that interact in logical space, having a life of their own at a remove from human existence. Instead, we must take seriously the Greek sense that inquiry into the structure of the universe and of the human mind is needed in order to comport oneself well. For an analytic philosopher with a dry wit, it is easy to make fun of a figure such as Thales for claiming that everything is water (and that souls are present in all things). "Presocratic inquiries were inevitably crude. Thales, if we are to believe the later testimony, held that everything is made of water," such that "cucumbers are 100 per cent water, not 99 per cent as modern culinary pundits say." As is all the sand in the Sahara Desert (Barnes 1987, 21).

By contrast, here is a vastly more imaginative classicist, namely Nietzsche:

> Greek philosophy seems to begin with an absurd notion, with the proposition that *water* is the primal origin and the womb of all things. Is it really necessary to take serious notice of this proposition? It is. . . . because contained in it, if only embryonically, is the thought, "all things are one." (Nietzsche 1962, 38–39).

Or take the notion that a cosmic principle of reason is echoed in the human mind, first articulated by Heraclitus. If one believes this, then the best life one can lead will be based upon abiding by that principle of reason. This illustrates how it could be that philosophical reflection can lead to insight about existence and its meaning, thus issuing in an exemplary way of living. Whatever may be said on behalf of philosophy as a merely academic enterprise, there are core questions of philosophy as it has existed in the Western tradition – most of them, of course, first examined by the ancient Greeks – that are not legitimately pursued in a manner that fails to take account of the individual to whom these questions pertain, and whose being is at stake in how she or he answers them. So there may be little to be said in favor of a nonexistential ideal of what philosophy ought to be.

We ought to reject the naysayers who assert, generally without argument, that the "view of philosophy as concerned with the philosophy of life" is in fact "rather narrow" (!) and too "romantic" besides (Hamlyn 1990, 13). What it is, in fact, is ambitious, inclusive, and ancient. It may be fair enough to claim, as

---

[11] Cf. Hadot (2002, 5–6).

Kierkegaard, Socrates, and the Meaning of Life

another analytically minded contemporary philosopher does (see Cooper 2012, 25), that "you could not make a life from thinking what Anaximander or Anaximenes did about the origins and current composition of the natural world," but he might have gone a bit out of his way to notice what Heidegger writes about the former (in Heidegger 2015, 1–77).

If we were to trace the existential spirit through philosophy's early flowering in ancient Greece and the broader Mediterranean world from Thales (and Sappho) to Pyrrho, we would find that it is pervasive during these centuries – yet more emphatically so at certain places and times. It is accurate to suggest that, just as it is centered geographically in Athens during its heyday, the existential spirit builds up to a pinnacle in the middle dialogues of Plato, above all in the figure of Socrates as he is presented in the *Phaedo*, discoursing about the psyche on the last day of his life. Nowhere else is intense theoretical reflection linked to such an urgent issue that concerns each of us in particular. Death is the only certainty, and the only thing about which nothing is more uncertain, as Kierkegaard points out, writing that "inasmuch as death is the object of earnestness," a sincere inquiry into it requires "that we should not be overhasty in acquiring an opinion with regard to it" (KW 15, 99–100). It must not be a *mere* opinion to which we pay lip-service, because "not only is that person mad who talks senselessly, but the person is fully as mad who states a correct opinion if it has absolutely no significance for him" (KW 15, 99–100). In Kierkegaard's pseudonymous *Concluding Unscientific Postscript*, this theme is much stressed.

According to Plato's *Apology*, Socrates – on trial for impiety and corruption – claimed that "the unexamined life is not worth living" for a human being,[12] and that he had a special vocation to provoke his fellow citizens into leading the examined life. Plato goes out of his way to indicate that he himself was present at the trial (34a, 38b), an uncharacteristic move that is not duplicated anywhere else in his writings. That would appear to suggest that we are getting something like an eyewitness account of what the historical Socrates said on this occasion.[13] That Kierkegaard supports this interpretation is shown, e.g., when he writes that "Socrates would not use the speech which was offered him," finding it too "artfully contrived."[14] In addition, the character of Socrates in the *Apology* is a literary figure who bears a strong resemblance to the historical philosopher.

---

[12] *Apology* 38a. Unless otherwise noted, all quotations are from the G. M. A. Grube translation of this dialogue (Indianapolis, IN: Hackett, 1981).

[13] Cf. Brickhouse and Smith (1989, 2–4). The judicious conclusion that this text is a reconstruction of the speech that Socrates actually gave is reached by Hadot (2002, 24). See also Cornford (1932, 35).

[14] Kierkegaard, *Pap* X 4 A 314 / JP 4283. Undated entry from 1851.

6   *The Philosophy of Søren Kierkegaard*

And Socrates must have been up to something, because his friend Chaerephon went to the Delphic oracle of Apollo and asked if anyone was wiser than Socrates. Perhaps it had to do with the widespread opinion "that in certain respects Socrates is superior to the majority" (34e–35a). The answer he received was that "no one was wiser" (21a). This prompted Socrates to search for others who seemed to possess wisdom – including politicians, poets, and craftsmen – in order to show the oracle a counterexample (21b–23b). Was he trying to refute the oracle? The overall tone of Socrates in this dialogue is that of a religiously devout person, so it seems more likely that he was seeking only to clarify, through an *apparent* counterexample, what exactly the oracle meant. Singling out the poets especially, Kierkegaard writes that poetry "present[s] things in the medium of the imagination instead of urging people toward ethical realization" (*Pap* X 2 A 229; NB14:55 / KJN 6, 381). Socrates, by contrast, "managed to keep himself on the pinnacle of continually expressing the existential,"[15] as the Danish existential thinker points out.

We get a glimpse of the Socratic method of questioning when Socrates cross-examines his accuser Meletus (24d–27e), leading him to contradict himself and to show that he does not really care about the issues of impiety and corruption. What is the pertinence of the latter point? If Socrates is guilty as charged, then it would seem to be irrelevant whether the plaintiff cares authentically about the matters at hand. Yet a central premise of the Socratic method is that the person being examined be truly invested in the views that he or she espouses, and not merely to be entertaining a position. His emphasis on the difference between theory abstractly conceived and actual personal conviction shows the existential spirit of Socratic philosophizing.

Philosophy for Socrates, then, is "a process, a discipline, a lifelong quest,"[16] based upon subjecting one's ideas to rational criticism in dialogue with others, refuting apparent knowledge in order to bring people to admit their ignorance and interrogate things more critically. Some of his interlocutors might find this edifying, but many others, such as Meletus, are only annoyed and angry to be roped into a conversation guided by Socrates and *his* agenda. How can Socrates defend the value of his practice? For one thing, he regards himself as divinely authorized to do what he has been doing, thanks in part to the oracle, even if he is a prophet with no message to proclaim – this is why Kierkegaard calls him "purely negative" (CI, 210). It is a magnificent refutation of the charge of impiety if he can convince the jury that he indeed has a sacrosanct vocation to engage in philosophical questioning: "the god ordered me," he says, to lead "the

---

[15] From the same 1849 notebook entry just quoted.
[16] Tarnas (1991, 34–35); see also Ricken (1991, 54).

Kierkegaard, Socrates, and the Meaning of Life

life of a philosopher" (28e). He is on a mission. "With respect to Socrates the difficulty is not to understand his teaching but to understand *him*" (*Pap* VIII 1 A 490; NB4:9 / KJN 4, 292).

He is not, as the plaintiffs contend, "a student of all things in the sky and below the earth, who makes the worse argument the stronger" (18b). He renounces naturalistic inquiry, and here too Kierkegaard echoes him. "If there were anything to be done through natural science in the process of defining spirituality, I'd be the first to get my hands on a microscope" (*Pap* 46 VII 1 A 191 / PJ, 240; trans. modified). Socrates attends to the human realm (26d), and within this realm he is not concerned with rhetorical expertise for its own sake, but with discovering the truth – insofar as that is an attainable goal. "I think there is no greater blessing for the city than my service to the god. For I go around doing nothing but persuading both young and old among you not to care for your body or your wealth [but] for the best possible state of your soul" (30a–b). He is "a kind of gadfly" (30e) who stings in order to jolt people out of their complacency, thus performing a valuable service to the city, as a divine messenger. In Kierkegaard's opinion, Socrates compares himself to a gadfly "because he want[s] to have only ethical significance."[17] He confers on each of his neighbors "what I say is the greatest benefit, by trying to persuade him not to care for any of [her or] his belongings before caring that he himself should be as good and as wise as possible" (36c). If there is a clear positive imperative to be found in Socrates' quest for wisdom, as outlined in the *Apology*, it is that we should focus on the state of our psyche, our mind or soul,[18] rather than on such external affairs as heaping up wealth. Inner riches are inestimably more valuable than outer ones.

One thing that seemed both sacrilegious and potentially corrupting to Socrates' accusers was that, in the words of Meletus, "he says that the sun is [made of] stone, and the moon earth" (26d). The prosecution has formally alleged that Socrates "busies himself studying things in the sky and below the earth" (19b). Yet this is a misconception, as not only Plato but also Aristotle attests,[19] a source of which is the comic drama *The Clouds*, by Aristophanes, to which Socrates alludes and refers (18c-d, 19c). This play shows a character named "Socrates" suspended in a basket, offering reductive physicalistic explanations such as that thunder is a vast, heavenly fart. Evidently, Socrates was associated with the natural philosophers in the popular imagination; yet, for Kierkegaard, it makes perfect sense: "How normal! First he occupies himself

---

[17] Journal entry from 1846 (*Pap* VII 1 A 69 / JP 4265).   [18] Cf. Stewart (2020, 213–214).
[19] See, e.g., *Metaphysics* 987b.

8 *The Philosophy of Søren Kierkegaard*

with nature (natural science, astronomy, etc.) and then goes over to dealing with [human beings] as an ethicist and stays with that" (*Pap* X 4 A 319 / JP 4284).

If the Socrates of Plato's *Apology* is concerned with finding a general understanding, it is of such topics as "virtue ... and those other things about which you hear me conversing and testing myself and others" (38a), such things presumably including beauty, goodness, equality, piety, and the like. As we shall see, Socrates seeks to define such terms. And he has no doubt that this is his existential task. To philosophize has been urged upon him "by means of oracles and dreams, and in every other way that a divine manifestation has ever ordered a person to do anything" (33c). This assurance of spiritual purpose is a major reason why it is that "belief in a special, direct relation between himself and divine forces must be accepted in any account of his mentality which lays claim to completeness."[20] Another, even more central, reason is Socrates' famous *daimon* or divine sign.

Socrates has a sacred inward "voice" which, he says, Meletus has ridiculed in the trial, which "began when I was a child" and "whenever it speaks it turns me away from something I was about to do" (31d; see also 40a–b). Also documented by Xenophon and Diogenes Laertius, the *daimonion* or *daimon* is mentioned in numerous other Platonic dialogues as well.[21] It is inwardly felt by Socrates as a kind of prompting, and interpreted as a religious inspiration to be trusted; when he figures out why it steered him as it did, this tends to be after the fact. Initially, as soon as the daimonic signal manifests itself, his duty is simply to obey – and, apparently, he always does.[22] No portrayal of Socrates can leave aside his *daimonion*, and Kierkegaard is an inspired genius in a similar manner. Yet the divine sign is considered by many interpreters to be an embarrassment for Socratic rationalism.

The admittedly "scientific" Russell, who complains about the "religious" character of the *Apology*, concludes his account of the *Phaedo* by refusing to name its author a philosopher because it contains arguments for the immortality of the psyche.[23] The *psuchē*, which is the Greek term for mind or soul, can be

---

[20] Guthrie (1971, 84).

[21] See, e.g., *Euthydemus* 272e, *Euthyphro* 3b, *Phaedrus* 242b-c, *Republic* 496c, *Theaetetus* 151a; *Theages* 128d; Diogenes Laertius II.32; Xenophon, *Apology* 13, *Memorabilia* I.1.2–4. On how for Socrates the *daimon* prevails over the dictates of autonomous, secular ratiocination, see McPherran (1996, 202–207).

[22] See McPherran (1996, 199): "The fact that daemonic warnings yield a kind of knowledge and are not mere subjective hunches is indicated by Socrates' full confidence that the *daimonion* is always caused by a divinity that would never purposefully mislead him." See also Brickhouse and Smith (1989, 250n): "We know of no case where Socrates receives a daimonic alarm but ignores it, or goes ahead and completes the action despite the warning."

[23] Russell (1972, 132–143). The *Phaedo* is both "religious" and "mystical," and Plato for writing it deserves to spend time in "scientific purgatory."

Kierkegaard, Socrates, and the Meaning of Life

adequately translated by any of these three terms and thematically dominates Plato's *Phaedo* – a dialogue that is, *contra* Russell, a philosophical as well as a literary masterpiece. It combines logical argument[24] and mythological speculation and presents Socrates simultaneously as an abstract theorist and an unforgettably singular person.

We have every reason to think that Socrates' belief in his "divine sign" was well-known, that it was a main basis for the charge of blasphemy, and that it was taken seriously by himself and by his contemporaries. So one way to proceed would be simply to leave it conspicuously out of one's depiction of Socrates in Plato's *Apology*, proclaiming that all we need know about "the divine nature" for the philosopher on trial is that it is "totally and perfectly rational,"[25] universal secular reason prevailing over anything particular to Socrates. Or, as an alternative, one could insist that Socrates' *daimonion* is only a way of denoting his human power of listening to the voice of reason.[26] Yet, at face value, the *Apology* could hardly be more explicit in confirming that Socrates viewed his philosophical activity as a sacred vocation, grounded in extra-rational sources of conviction.[27] Most importantly for present purposes, while Socrates advocates the examined life for any human being, his intense pursuit of that life is based on a directive that is uniquely his own. As Kierkegaard sums it up in 1851, "Socrates believed that he was divinely commissioned" (*Pap* X 4 A 334 / JP 4286).

Although his "relentless honesty" is "easily mistaken for arrogance,"[28] and some readers will claim that calling Socrates arrogant is spot on, he is a warrior of thought, willing to die for the sake of his philosophical mission, God's gift to the city (30a, 31a), who has begun something that will not end with his own death (39c-d). Even an ambivalent interpreter of Socrates such as Nietzsche admits that, for Socrates, "thinking serves life,"[29] and his admirer Kierkegaard

---

[24] As Kierkegaard says, Socrates in a sense – or at some moments – "is actually a martyr to the numerical" (*Pap* X 2 A 449 / JP 4277).

[25] Cooper (2012, 39). I find no mention of the Socratic *daimon* anywhere in the dozens of pages which are devoted to the Socratic way of life in this study; only such assertions as that to follow in Socrates' legacy is to live from "rationally worked out, rationally grasped, and rationally defended, reasoned ideas about the world and one's place in it" – Cooper (2012, 17).

[26] See Nusssbaum (1980); see also Nussbaum (1985). It is worth adding that both Cooper and Nussbaum endorse philosophy as a way of life as a Socratic ideal – see Cooper (2012, 29) and Nussbaum (1994, 4). So if they regard Socrates' *daimonion* as a thing to be swept under the rug, it is not for the sake of disparaging his existential imperative to philosophize.

[27] See McPherran (1996, 177, 194, 210). All this is *contra* Gregory Vlastos (1991, 157–178, 223–232); and also *contra* Nussbaum (1995), where Socrates is recruited as a neoliberal secular rationalist.

[28] Nails (2009, 331–332).

[29] Nietzsche (2001b, 145). Cf. Nietzsche (1979b, 127): "Simply to acknowledge the fact: *Socrates* is so close to me that I am almost continually fighting with him." It is Socrates' "adamant denial

10 *The Philosophy of Søren Kierkegaard*

agrees in no uncertain terms that the ancient Athenian is someone for whom "theory and practice" are fully harmonious (CI, 51). Furthermore, whatever wisdom he might gain in this lifelong quest is not attained once-and-for-all, since its pursuit and maintenance require a kind of "perpetual self-examination" in conversation with others.[30] By condemning Socrates to be executed, his fellow citizens are only harming themselves, converting their unappreciated beneficiary into a martyr for his cause.

Or so he asserts, in his defense at the trial. Yet other Socratic dialogues by Plato paint a less consistently commendable picture. Take, for instance, the *Crito*, which purports to relay the discussion that the eponymous close friend of Socrates had with him after sneaking into prison to rescue him as he was awaiting the administering of the death penalty. Crito, who has been trying to persuade Socrates to escape, makes what is apparently his last effort to do so; bribes have been paid (43a), and the leadership of Athens is willing to look the other way if Socrates' friends want to smuggle him out of jail and save his life. Crito argues (44b–c) that allowing Socrates to be put to death will deprive him of an irreplaceable companion, a loss that will sting more painfully as other people assume that Crito did not try hard enough to rescue him from this fate. Moreover, it is not inherently just for Socrates to accept the death penalty after a blatantly unjust court case in which a greater majority of jurors voted for his execution than had found him guilty (45c–d), and if he consents to die, he will be failing as a father to raise and educate his sons.[31]

Hearing these four reasons for escape, Socrates does not bother to reply to more than one of them, the second, which he reduces to a superficial concern for public gossip, answering his devoted friend with a cruel rhetorical question about whether we should worry about what "the majority" think (44c–d, 48a), full stop.[32] He does not respond to Crito's exasperation that all of this, including the trial itself, could have been avoided, or Crito's insinuation that he is taking the easy way out, all too willing to injure his family and friends and end his

---

of the passions," which as we shall see is found elsewhere in Plato, that largely explains Nietzsche's later polemics against him, as is noted by Evans (2017, 27).

[30] Yonezawa (2004, 21–22).

[31] On why Socrates' death might qualify as a suicide, see Frey (1978). Also, already in the *Apology* he shows a rather peculiar attitude toward his three sons – when he asks those who voted for his acquittal not to look after them out of loyalty to Socrates himself, but rather only to "reproach them as I reproach you, [if] they do not care for the right things" (41d).

[32] See Beversluis (2000, 64–66). Cf. Weiss (1998, 81): while acknowledging that Crito shows great devotion in his love for his friend, she nevertheless convicts him of having "unphilosophical and utterly conventional views." For Woozley (1979, 17), it is only due to Crito's "muddleheadedness in argument" that he even mentions how much he and other friends of Socrates will miss him.

Kierkegaard, Socrates, and the Meaning of Life

philosophical career at a premature date. Instead, he detours into a bizarre report of a dialogue he supposedly had with the personified Laws of Athens (50a–54c), to the effect that he has implicitly signed a sort of social contract with these laws over the course of his entire life. This rhetorical flourish is not convincing to Crito at all; it only leaves him in devastated silence (54d), as if his friend Socrates is not someone with whom one can reason once he has dug in his heels. This is not an instance of simply following the argument wherever it leads – rather, it looks like obstinacy.

Yet even in his assurance about accepting the death penalty, Socrates gives an impression of being remarkably at peace with himself and his situation. A healthy stubbornness is probably needed in order to sustain the kind of conviction he shows in the *Apology*, motivated to enact the "divine mission" of philosophy not only by the Delphic oracle's mysterious pronouncement but also and especially by his inward belief in "a private daimonic voice."[33] While we must at times ask ourselves whether Socrates lives up to his ideals, those ideals are nothing less than a notion of philosophy as an existentially urgent way of life, a profoundly committed quest for wisdom involving the utmost care for one's soul.[34] Despite the unmistakably social dimension of his project as Athenian gadfly, he seems in the *Apology* to regard the realm of law and politics as quite an alienating space into which his particular subjectivity does not fit – which is why he sees his nonappearance in court until age seventy as a sign of his honesty (17d–18a). Defiant toward the jury at his trial, Socrates is surprisingly acquiescent in submitting to his legal penalty.

Although Socrates seems sure that his way of life "is the best ... for all human beings," as Nehamas points out, we are also following in a Socratic spirit if we conceive of philosophy as "an effort to develop a mode of life that is unique to [each] particular individual."[35] A manifesto for the examined life, his defense in Plato's *Apology* is intent upon distinguishing his concern for human existence from the more naturalistic inquiries of some of his predecessors (19c, 26d) such as Anaxagoras, who shares with Socrates the distinction of being accused of impiety and brought to trial in Athens, from which Anaxagoras was subsequently exiled.[36] We are struck by the extraordinary personality of Socrates, and the impression it has left on other thinkers from Plato through the present day. Tranquil in facing death, professing to know nothing yet assured of esoteric insights, and having the brazenness to claim that the "penalty" he truly deserves is to be provided with banquets at public expense

---

[33] Weiss (1998, 15–16). See also Brickhouse and Smith (1989, 87).

[34] Cf. Peperzak (2003, 16).   [35] Alexander Nehamas (1998, 196–197).

[36] See Diogenes Laertius II.12–14.

12   *The Philosophy of Søren Kierkegaard*

(36d–37a), Socrates has been an inspiration to many. Yet Kierkegaard suggests that Socrates is "*essentially* unpopular," for few "in each generation" can "understand that an idea could sway a [person] to such an extent that" they will die for it (*Pap* VIII 1 A 491; NB4:10 / DSK, 122). Although he can be quite infuriating, he looms so large at the dawn of Greek philosophy that those like Heraclitus who came before him have come to be known as pre-Socratics, as if they occupied a prehistoric era. But philosophy was already in the air, which is why Socrates could be conflated with other philosophers, and to some degree he was made into a scapegoat for the threat that they posed to conventional values. He has been called the first existential thinker.

Not only did Socrates turn away from naturalistic inquiry but he also spurned a cultural form of materialism that involved valuing money more than the state of one's soul (see 29e–30b, 36c). The jurors who convicted him were people who "[did] not care for the right things" (41e). Although he alienates some nonreligious readers with his stress on having a spiritual vocation, Socrates is more than anything an advocate for the reflective life, a hero for philosophy hereafter. He does not inquire for the sake of gaining abstract knowledge, but aims at a wisdom that could inform concrete practice, caring for the self and urging others to do the same, devoting his entire life to this endless task.[37] It requires nothing less than a fanatical passion for scientific rationality to protest (*way* too much!) that to emulate Socrates is to govern one's life by "rationally worked out, rationally grasped, and rationally defended, reasoned ideas about the world";[38] in fact, if a prophet is someone who carries a divinely ordained message, Socrates qualifies as a prophet in the spirit of the Abrahamic faiths. Countless ancient thinkers and schools of thought trace their origin to him as their founding instigator. And Kierkegaard, as we have seen, did name Socrates as his only prototype.

When Bob Dylan's third full-length studio album was released in 1964, it was entitled *Another Side of Bob Dylan*, in a probably unconscious allusion to Kierkegaard – the point at the time being that this was a less politically focused and more personal collection of songs. It is an oft-repeated platitude that Kierkegaard's pseudonymous *Concluding Unscientific Postscript* is either the main or the only place where "subjective truth" is talked about. The misconception that "explicit remarks" in Kierkegaard's corpus about how subjectivity and

---

[37] Cf. Muench (2010a, 18–19n). On how Socrates can sound "more [like] a religious visionary than a philosopher," see also Murchland (2008, 10).

[38] Cooper (2012, 17). Regarding Socrates as a prophet, see Ghaffari (2011). To impose our currently fashionable notions of rationality upon the ancient Greeks, as Cooper does, is to deprive ourselves of one of the most beneficial features of studying ancient thought – namely, that it provokes us to think beyond contemporary norms.

Kierkegaard, Socrates, and the Meaning of Life

objectivity are related "is [*sic*] almost exclusively the domain of the *Concluding Unscientific Postscript*" is defended by one scholar, for instance.[39] Yet it is not in the *Postscript* but a year earlier, in 1845's *Three Discourses on Imagined Occasions*, that this terminology originates.

> One can have an opinion about remote events, about a natural object, about nature, about scholarly works, about another human being, and so on about much else, and when one expresses this opinion the wise person can decide whether it is correct or incorrect. No one, however, troubles the opinion-holder with a consideration of *another side of the truth* [my emphasis], whether one actually does have the opinion, whether it is just something one is reciting. Yet this other side is just as important, because not only is that person mad who talks nonsensically, but the person is fully as mad who states a correct opinion if it has absolutely no signifi-cance for him.... It is so easy, so very easy, to acquire a true opinion, and yet it is so difficult to have an opinion and to have it in truth. (KW 15, 99–100)

This alludes forward to a number of sustained discussions in the *Postscript*, as we shall see in due time.

We are temporal, finite beings, "and this means that there is a fundamental contingency, uncertainty, and unpredictability in our existence" (Damgaard 2007, 201). Any divine calling – such as that of Socrates or Kierkegaard – is issued, in the latter's terms, to "the single individual" (*den Enkelte*). Therefore, an approach to religion "that takes numerical form" is only a "deceit" (NB23: 11 / KJN 8, 209).

"We look before and after, / And pine for what is not," Shelley laments in "To a Skylark," and yet it is precisely through a backward glance that we are given what in Plato's *Phaedo* is viewed by Socrates as one of the most compelling reasons to look forward to our immortality. Echoing the *Meno* and alluding to its arguments, Socrates about one-third of the way into the *Phaedo* arrives at the robust conclusion that our minds "existed apart from the body before they took on human form, and they had intelligence" (76c). How does he justify this claim? There is, as Cebes asserts and others agree, an "excellent argument" that when someone is "interrogated in the right manner," they "always give the right answer ... and they could not do this if they did not possess the knowledge" within them, in some sense (73a; see *Meno* 82b–86b). In order to notice that two sticks we see are nearly equal in length, or not at all equal, we call to mind – that is, we *recall* – an ideal standard of equality to which we refer the sticks we perceive (74d–75c).[40] Likewise with finding things holy, or just, or beautiful.

---

[39] Turnbull (2015, 2).

[40] See, e.g., Adamson (2014, 138–139); Burger (1984, 77). Cf. Nightingale (2021, 122); see Ebrey (2023, 103): the argument from *Phaedo* 73c-77d can be mapped out as follows: equality itself is

We must have been acquainted with ideal standards of these as well, so that we can recollect them and appeal to them in making judgments of holiness, or justice, or beauty. These are not spatial or temporal, but intellectually apprehensible: as Socrates asks (65d), "Have you ever seen any of these things with your eyes?" The reply is: of course not. They are invisible and always the same, and the psyche that grasps them is understood "just as abstractly as the pure essence of the things that are the object of its activity," as Kierkegaard points out (CI, 68–72). According to this dialogue, though, being and knowledge are intertwined in such a manner that both of these have existential relevance: as a recent scholar contends, "if Platonism is otherworldly, it is also committed to the relevance of the otherworldly to *this* world" (Gerson 2020, 261). The best life for a human being is one that strives toward knowing what is real. Kierkegaard would add that this must include actuality – not only eternal essences.

Those who practice philosophy "in the right way" (69c–d) are regarded by Socrates as initiates into a higher insight, enlightened beings who have purified themselves to obtain access to the truth. Though here an ambiguity enters. On one side, the lover of wisdom who "must," as Socrates avows in the *Euthyphro*, "follow his beloved wherever it may lead him" (14c), seems doomed in the *Phaedo* to a sadly unrequited love. The enlightenment sought is not to be found during life in this world. Illustrating the "bloodless abstraction" that Nietzsche complains about, the denigration of sensory experience,[41] Socrates argues that our bodily senses can *only* deceive us: we do not "find any truth in sight or hearing," and the mind "reasons best when none of these senses troubles it, neither hearing nor sight, nor pain nor pleasure, but when it is most by itself, taking leave of the body and as far as possible having no contact or association with it in its search for reality" (65b–d); a true philosopher will approach "each pure reality by itself" with "thought alone" (66a). But does our embodied experience *always* deceive us? Is not Socrates' geometric diagram in the *Meno* an aid to learning an abstract truth about the square, and does not the sight of nearly equal things or the hearing of somewhat beautiful sounds bring to mind the respective forms of equality and beauty?[42] According to Socrates, "either we can never attain knowledge" or we can do so wholly and completely "after death," condemned during this life to "be closest to knowledge if we refrain as much as possible from association with the body" (66e–67a). Yet the

---

discrete from roughly equal things; since we refer to this standard of equality in this life but do not encounter it as such, we must have gained knowledge of it at some point; we could only have gained this knowledge before we were born, then forgotten it, so that in this life it needs to be "recollected."

[41] Nietzsche (1962, 69–79).

[42] See Gordon (1999, 141–142): "The two realms [of pure reason and sensory experience] are necessarily linked, and philosophical inquiry into the nature of reality must necessarily take place within the realm of appearances."

Kierkegaard, Socrates, and the Meaning of Life

dialogue bears witness, through its own examples, to the way that our embodied sensory perceptions can lead to knowledge – however imperfect this might be.

The deductive arguments in the *Phaedo* are persuasive, to the degree that they are, mainly in light of the metaphysical picture that Socrates and his friends tacitly accept. And this picture does have its austere appeal. Our perception of more or less equal things summons to mind a perfect ideal of equality: in *seeing* approximately equal sticks, we *think* of this perfect standard.[43] Likewise, we ourselves may be imperfect in measuring up to the *Phaedo*'s standard of asceticism – Socrates, after all, warns against bodily desire yet has three sons, one of them an infant – but the ideal can still exert its alluring pull on us. To a significant degree, Socrates is depicted as an extraordinary being, whose invisible soul is motivated by no emotion stronger than a passionate longing to attain truth,[44] and who compared to other human beings is "a rational soul temporarily housed in a body and awaiting release,"[45] in the language of Pythagorean mysteries. The zenith of asceticism functions as a regulative ideal, guiding us toward becoming unafraid of a death that amounts to the freeing of the psyche from its bodily confinement; insofar as we feel afraid of this prospect, it is as if we have "a child in us" (77e–78a), and need someone to sing a charm over us to alleviate our fear.

Remarkably, Socrates does not scorn the admitted need for a "charmer." It could be that rational argumentation itself functions as a kind of song that we sing to ourselves, because it fails to prove conclusively that the mind or soul is immortal.[46] The best it can do is to offer something like an analogy. "Consider," Socrates says, "whether it follows from all that has been said that the soul is most like the divine, deathless, intelligible, uniform, indissoluble, always the same as itself, whereas the body is most like that which is human, mortal, multiform, unintelligible," and "never consistently the same" (80a–b). His colleagues are in agreement with this characterization and with the ensuing conclusion that a philosopher's purified psyche will go its own way when the body dies, surviving as it were in another realm,[47] even though this itself is a sort of poetical metaphor, since the realm in which geometric shapes exist is

---

[43] See Bedu-Addo (1991, 38–42). On Socrates' asceticism and its limitations, see Nussbaum (1986, 151–152). On his "nihilism," due to the dialogues that end in *aporia*, see Söderquist (2010, 189).

[44] And also, as Kierkegaard notes, a pre-Cartesian fear of being deceived: "Being in error was what Socrates feared most of all" (*Pap* VII 1 A 193; NB:80 / KJN 4, 68).

[45] Beversluis (2000, 73). Regarding the philosopher's "passionate desire for truth," see Grube (1958, 129). With regard to the Pythagorean echoes about our imprisonment in a body, see *Phaedo* 59e, 62b; Horky (2013, 172–173).

[46] As Kierkegaard discerns: see *Pap* X 3 A 315; JP 4280. "Socrates could not prove the immortality of the soul."

[47] Cf. Nightingale (2021, 50–53, 118–119).

16   *The Philosophy of Søren Kierkegaard*

not literally a place. The "rational psychology" of the *Phaedo*, as Schopenhauer points out, is motivated primarily by a concern for the immortality of the psyche thus understood.[48] Yet the abstract essences the philosopher will contemplate with her purified mind alone are vividly described as objects of powerful sensuous apprehension. They are beyond concrete perception, but somehow *beautiful*:[49] "Those who have purified themselves sufficiently by philosophy live in the future altogether without a body; they make their way to even more beautiful dwelling places which it is hard to describe" (114c; see also 110d–e). This way of thinking is present when Keats contemplates the images on an ancient Greek urn and writes: "Heard melodies are sweet, but those unheard / Are sweeter; therefore, ye soft pipes, play on; / Not to the sensual ear, but, more endeared, / Pipe to the spirit ditties of no tone." Sensible beauty hints at a beauty that transcends the senses. The human mind is a divine faculty, capable of knowing the truth about ultimate reality, beyond time and change. And, since the philosopher has identified herself with her capacity for pure reason, *she* herself can perhaps survive bodily death in a dwelling place too beautiful to describe. Kierkegaard's pseudonym "Johannes Climacus" calls this *Salighed*, "eternal happiness" (CUP, 19 and *passim*).

So the argument from recollection gives reason to believe that the mind must have always existed, and that it was in some unspecified manner capable of contemplating pure forms. Then the enumeration of the psyche's affinity *to* those pure forms provides further assurance that it like them has a nonbodily kind of existence. It fits with the outlook these arguments prescribe, then, to conclude as Socrates does that what is especially bad about powerful embodied experiences of pain or pleasure, which include many or most of our emotions, is that they make us convinced *in our soul* that we are experiencing something real and true (83c–d).[50] This leads us to pursue these things and take them seriously, even building our lives around such pursuits, to the detriment of the philosophical life, and of our mind's perfection. A philosopher's mind, by contrast, "achieves a calm from such emotions," focusing on what is akin to itself (84a). This is what it means to "absorb truth and make it one's own" (*Pap* IV A 87 / PJ, 155). The less composed, more hysterical Kierkegaard nevertheless learned from Socrates and on his death bed seemed to be at peace.

We cannot be certain that our mind or soul survives death, but we have reason to hope so. Yet two of Socrates' companions, Simmias and Cebes, demand

---

[48] Schopenhauer (1974, 43). With regard to what follows, see Nehamas (1975, 111).

[49] See Nightingale (2021, 163). See also Tarnas (1991, 34): "Words could indeed distort and deceive, . . . but words could also point, as to a precious invisible mystery, to something genuine and enduring. To find one's way to that genuine reality was the task confronting the philosopher."

[50] See, e.g., Trabattoni (2023, 7, 74).

Kierkegaard, Socrates, and the Meaning of Life 17

further persuasion, the latter claiming that a philosopher who faces death with confidence would be "foolish" unless she "can prove that the soul is altogether immortal" (88b), and the former also offers considerations which undermine this belief. The exchange causes a hush of doubt to settle over the room, and the dialogue even reverts to its framing narrative, where the eyewitness Phaedo is telling a friend about Socrates' last day. How could Socrates respond, in order to address the uncertainties of his interlocutors? Phaedo says that he has never more fully admired Socrates than at this moment (88e–89a), in the gentleness and thoughtful care he shows in responding to his friends, respecting their state of mind even if he does not share their doubts. To the reader, this must be striking. Socrates – who is professing and, unmistakably, practicing a doctrine of calm with respect to human emotions such as the fear of death – takes evident pity on his friends and honors their perplexities. This is despite the fact that Socrates is soon to go gentle into that good night.

Here as always, then, the *Phaedo* is more than the sum of its arguments. If we attend to what might be called the poetics of the text, we notice a striking gesture. When the conversation about the nature of the psyche pauses at this moment of doubt, Socrates affectionately reaches out to caress Phaedo's hair, "for he was in the habit of playing with my hair at times," and says that the next day, "you will probably cut this" as a sign of mourning (89a–b). Socrates shows a deep concern for what his friends will be experiencing right after he is gone, and he tells them that it is *today* that they all ought to cut their hair in grief if they cannot rally themselves back to believing in the mind's immortality. Displaying once again the element of faith involved in seeking the truth, Socrates claims that his companions should be on guard against losing faith in discourse and ultimately "be deprived of truth and knowledge of reality" (90d).[51] For becoming distrustful toward argumentation, for instance because one has been convinced that the soul is immortal but then subsequently given reason to doubt this, could lead one to the despairing conclusion that we cannot find the truth, or even that there is no truth whatsoever. Socrates respects the fears and uncertainties of his friends but pushes back against them simultaneously.

In the interest of showing his companions why he is unafraid, he provides them with a narrative fragment of intellectual autobiography, beginning with the admission that, as a young man, he "was wonderfully keen on that wisdom which they call natural science" (96a), wanting to learn the explanation of everything. In this context, Anaxagoras is named again, as offering the promise of explaining through Mind why things are as they are; Socrates found this more

---

[51] See, e.g., Ahrensdorf (1995, 143). Am I the only one who hears an echo, as it were, of William James's famous essay "The Will to Believe"?

18   *The Philosophy of Søren Kierkegaard*

adequate than strictly material accounts (97b–98d). However, his "hope was dashed" when he discovered that Anaxagoras actually relied more often than not on physical descriptions, leaving Mind (*nous*) out of the picture.[52] Anaxagoras would typically give a reductive explanation of why Socrates is sitting in prison, rather than mentioning "the true causes," that Socrates thought it best to accept the death penalty, but this is insufficient, because his "sinews and bones" would have been in a distant land by now if he had decided to run away (98e–99a). Socrates developed a different, humanistic method: he began "to investigate the truth of things by means of words" (99e), with reference in each case to the true cause or reason (*aitia*),[53] arriving at a meaningful rather than mechanistic interpretation of phenomena. And this led him to venture faith in the real existence of the things such as goodness and beauty that are essential to such interpretations – an idealistic belief that he is still upholding.

This instills confidence in Socrates. Not only is the human psyche akin to these abstract essences, as Kierkegaard notes (CI, 68–69),[54] but it is also of its very nature to be alive and not to admit death (105c–e), any more than fire will admit coldness or snow will admit heat (103c–e). Rather, when death approaches, as it were, the psyche must either retreat from it and remain alive or else be destroyed. "Which?" one commentator asks, expressing doubt:[55] yet, to Socrates' credit, he does not insist that every reasonable person must share his belief that the mind or soul is necessarily alive. Indeed, he says this of his entire sequence of arguments:

> No sensible man would insist that these things are as I have described them, but I think it is fitting for a man to risk the belief – for the risk is a noble one – that this, or something like this, is true of our souls and their dwelling places, for the soul is [clearly] immortal, and a man should repeat this to himself as if it were an incantation. (114d)

For the noble risk that it is "worth the effort to venture to believe" in the mind's immortality, he is lauded as an existential hero by Kierkegaard in his

---

[52] Cf. Gerson (2020, 48–51). See also Hartle (1986, 16): "Socrates is completely untroubled on the day of his death." This makes him appear "inhuman, extraordinary. That is, [he] seems to be either above or below the human, more than human or so grossly insensitive as to be monstrous."

[53] Kanayama (2000, 87): "The most important lesson to be learned from Socrates' experiences is the view that the good is the real *aitia*; actually this must be what Plato learned from Socrates' life in pursuit of the good."

[54] "The soul is here understood just as abstractly as the pure essence of the things that are the object of its activity."

[55] Hamlyn (1990, 51). More optimistic is Ebrey (2023, 260–263). Excessively pessimistic, because relying only upon *The Concept of Irony*, is Söderquist (2010), who describes Socrates as "nihilistic."

Kierkegaard, Socrates, and the Meaning of Life

dissertation (CI, 108–109) – and even more emphatically in his pseudonymous *Concluding Unscientific Postscript*, where "Johannes Climacus" writes: "If someone searches objectively for immortality and another invests the passion of the infinite in the uncertainty – where then is there more truth and who has the greater certainty?" After asking this, he answers:

> Socrates! He submits the question in what is objectively a problematic way: *if* there is an immortality. [But] he invests his entire life in this "if there is." He dares to die, and with the passion of the infinite he has so ordered his entire life as to make it likely that it must be so – *if* there is an immortality. Is there any better proof of the immortality of the soul?[56] (CUP, 169–170)

Nothing has been decisively proven at the end of the *Phaedo*; nonetheless, the combination of "faith and persuasive argument" endorsed at 70c may be sufficiently convincing that we, like Pascal, risk taking this stance. Simmias is right to have "some private misgivings," Socrates concedes – yet he adds that, if a person analyzes the matter adequately, he will "follow the argument as far as [one] can and if the conclusion is clear, you will look no further" (107a–b). For Socrates as for Kierkegaard, the demands of reason give way to personal commitment.

At the outset of the dialogue, Socrates was released from the shackles that had bound his ankles (59e–60c); now, as he prepares to drink the poison and to be released from this life, going to live "altogether without a body" and making his way "to even more beautiful dwelling places which it is hard to describe" (114c), his friends reflect that it felt "as if we had lost a father and would be orphaned for the rest of our lives" (116a). Although Plato's text, at face value, offers the sad comfort that "Socrates' companions do not need him" in order to practice "philosophy, which they will still have after he departs,"[57] the words he puts into Phaedo's mouth about losing a father and being orphans forever after are heartrending enough to undercut this all-too-rational view. We readily identify with Socrates' friends when they burst out sobbing as he drains the hemlock (117c–d), aware that his death constitutes a real loss. Is it a loss for them only or perhaps for Socrates himself as well? Supposedly, he is on his way to encounter ultimate reality, in the company of other purified philosophical minds,[58] yet no one can be certain of this.

---

[56] Cf. Gordon, 1999, 38–40. As she points out, despite the "air of fallibility surrounding Socrates' beliefs," we observe here not doubt but "Socrates' deep commitment to beliefs, and to a way of life" led in accord with them. "Beliefs are vessels on which we navigate the dangerous waters of human existence," and commitment to beliefs about the soul's indestructibility is justified for existential reasons, that we will live better with these beliefs.

[57] Ebrey (2023, 193).

[58] See Topping (2007, 30–31), on the company of fellow philosophers that Socrates will presumably enjoy after death. On the "life-guiding beliefs" that concern him in this text see Peterson (2011, 193).

20 *The Philosophy of Søren Kierkegaard*

Nonetheless, Socrates stakes his very existence on the life-guiding hope that his psyche will survive among the very entities whose definitions he was asking for in earlier dialogues such as the *Euthyphro*. While no longer the agnostic that he was in the *Apology*, his views about the likelihood of an afterlife are bracketed by disclaimers as to their demonstrative truth, and require stories such as the myth of the underworld (107e–114b) to render them more vivid and cogent. The philosopher's way of living requires courage that aiming toward the goal of immortality is actually the most appropriate manner to come to terms with our finitude: courage, that is, which is formed and maintained against the background of fear that we would otherwise suffer if we were to believe that bodily death brings about the annihilation of consciousness.

Socrates drinks the poisoned cup as "festively as if it were a delight" (*Pap* X 4 A 467 / JP 4288). As the numbness caused by the hemlock poison creeps from his feet and legs up to his belly and chest, however, Socrates with his last words tells Crito that they owe a debt that must be repaid by sacrificing a rooster to the god of healing (118a). Whereas impertinent critics from Nietzsche to present-day authors of footnotes hasten to proclaim that what Socrates *obviously* means is that life is an illness and dying the cure,[59] it seems to me much more likely that what Socrates is talking about is the fear of death. He *already* owes a debt to Asclepius because, with his last breath, he can report as a matter of fact that he is unafraid. The philosopher's heroism is never more evident than it is at this instant; he has been successfully cured of his fear.

In the *Apology* we see Socrates narrate his idiosyncratic account of how his vocation to practice philosophy was born – of a cryptic line from the Delphic Oracle and a more mysterious inner voice, followed by Socrates' attempt to figure out the meaning of these. His interpretation of the oracle and *daimon* led him to a strong assurance of a divinely sanctioned mission in his life. What may be most striking about the *Phaedo* is that, in the later dialogue, Socrates turns to an abstract philosophical question, the nature and destiny of the psyche, and demonstrates just as firm a conviction about this topic – with implications not unique to him but relevant to all of us. His aptitude for forming assurance is deployed in the defense of a theoretical hypothesis. This remarkably unites the Socrates of the *Apology*, sure only of his own purpose, with the Socrates who, in the *Phaedo*, is mapping out ambitious metaphysical positions about the mind as well as epistemological claims about what can be known – not to mention theories about the possibility of philosophical reflection itself, and its value for us human beings.

---

[59] Nietzsche (1997b, 12–17).

Kierkegaard, Socrates, and the Meaning of Life 21

It is here, in "Plato's most dualistic dialogue,"[60] that Socrates stands out above all as the paradigmatic existential thinker: he is working out his own views, not remaining theory-free or following an established doctrine, and he is doing so even as his mortality weighs urgently upon him. He has dedicated his life to the pursuit of wisdom and is ready to die for this pursuit, the poison awaiting him at the end of the day. His "divine" psyche (80b) is ready to ascend into an extraordinarily beautiful realm (114c), populated by that which is beyond change – that which "always is" (see Heidegger 2008, 86: the "meaning of Being for the Greeks" is *everlasting persistence*"). No wonder this quest was worthy of someone on a mission from the divine. Nowhere else does the love of wisdom shine quite so brightly as that which makes human life meaningful and worth living. What Socrates is presented as having discovered in the *Phaedo* – with the ostensibly absent Plato (59b) lurking behind every line in this literary gem of a text – is a way of transforming oneself with an eye on heaven, not as an object of wishful thinking (90d) but with sound if contestable reasons, having sought clarity about the psyche through an honest and sincere inquiry. That Socrates dies utterly without fear is the supreme vindication of the philosophical way of life.

As the verse etched into Kierkegaard's gravestone in Copenhagen's *Assistens Kierkegård* – yes, the literal meaning of his surname in Danish is "churchyard" – would appear to indicate, with its lines about lying in a bed of roses and speaking perpetually with Jesus, in all probability Søren Kierkegaard himself was no less convinced than Socrates was that part of him, his soul, would survive bodily death.[61] At least, this is what he hoped for: the life of the world to come. Nor was this merely an Averroean active intellect, or the soul bearing an "eternal watermark" as do all contingent beings created by God (WL, 89). It was Kierkegaard in his very *haecceity* – or "this-ness," in his utmost particularity and distinctiveness,[62] the specific self who he was meant by God to be and who actualized himself in space and temporality.

---

[60] Nails (2009, 335). It is also, as she adds, the only dialogue in which Plato's absence is (59b) explicitly remarked upon. On Socrates as exemplifying the philosophical life that involves faith as well as critical reasoning, see Dilman (1992, 14–17).

[61] Cf. Marino (2001, 61–75). See also Buben (2016, 46–64). For a competing view see Harrison Hall (1984). Buben links what I am calling the self bearing an "eternal watermark" with the notion of "dying to the world," which is all over the place, i.e., *passim*, in Kierkegaard's late work. On Socrates turning Christian, see Mooney (2007, 37–60).

[62] See Krishek (2022, 34–35, 52–53), with appropriate reference to Gerard Manley Hopkins; on her exceptional book, see Furtak (2024).

22 *The Philosophy of Søren Kierkegaard*

The author of a modern book called *Philosophy and the Meaning of Life* writes, "a man cannot be said to believe in Judgement Day unless he *lives for it*" (Britton 1969, 208). He adds that this "is the kind of confidence that a man [or woman] cannot fully explain: it meets needs of which he is not wholly conscious: it is a stance which he can take and which he is lost if he does not take" (Britton 1969, 213). Kierkegaard remarks in one of his Lily and Bird Discourses (on Matthew 6:24–34) that this is the real either/or: "either *God* – or, well, then the rest is unimportant" (KW 18, 21). He bids us to believe "that God cares for you" (KW 18, 43), to trust, with Nietzsche's Zarathustra, that "the world is deep,"[63] that is, that there is an underlying meaning to whatever transpires in time. (This ostensibly atheistic but religion-obsessed author wrote youthful poems to an unknown God.)[64] Socrates, during his trial and on the final day of his life (as creatively imagined by Plato), evinces the subjective belief – Kant or Blake might call it *persuasion* – which is the Kierkegaardian "other side of the truth."

Furthermore, his most Socratic figure, "Johannes Climacus" in the *Postscript*,[65] is also preoccupied with this topic. In proffering their diverse accounts of reality and knowledge, most philosophers or "speculative thinkers" have been "wholly indifferent to subjectivity" (CUP, 64). They are alike in being governed by the assumption that we must transcend our distinctive standpoint in order to find the truth, so they attempt to describe being and knowing in such a way as to eliminate the human perspective. "Objective thought," in the words of Merleau-Ponty, is "unaware of the subject" (2002, 240). Anticipating Husserl's criticism of "objective-scientific ways of thinking" (1970, 129), Kierkegaard as well as his pseudonym Climacus inveigh against "objective thinking" that is "not the least bit concerned about the thinker" (JJ:344 / KJN 2, 233). Those are Kierkegaard's own words, yet he is echoed by Climacus, who claims repeatedly that "subjectivity is truth" (e.g., CUP 171). If too "abstract" or "pure" a notion of existence is philosophically taken for granted, then the existing individual will not get clear about "what it means for him to be there" (CUP 159–160), to *be-in-the-world*. For the existential philosopher, who is concerned with the kind of "edifying truth" that hopefully can inform a life in pursuit of wisdom, the "truth which builds up" is the only "truth for you" that is worthy of the name (CUP 215; KW 4, 324). This truth does not and cannot aspire to the precision of a mathematical proof. It requires the passionate, love-based interest of the person to whose life it pertains. Following in the footpath of Socrates involves realizing that our life prior to doing philosophy has largely

---

[63] Nietzsche (2006, 133, 181, 261, 264).   [64] See Barrett (1958, 186–187).

[65] Cf. Muench (2010b), who calls Climacus a Socratic author par excellence.

Kierkegaard, Socrates, and the Meaning of Life

been wasted, and hence that "a change of priorities is needed," which will "make life worth living"[66] henceforth.

In the remaining sections of this Element, we will be dealing in an explicit and sustained manner with Kierkegaard's (life and) writings, yet the example of Socrates will be continuing to haunt us, as it haunted Kierkegaard. For Socrates does not only represent the kind of "negative" freedom that amounts to "arbitrariness" (CI, 228); instead, he exemplifies "true earnestness," in which "the subject no longer arbitrarily decides . . . but feels the task to be something that he has not assigned himself but that has been assigned to him" (CI, 235). As Kierkegaard also felt.

2 "Religiousness lies in being deeply moved": Love and Passionate Inspiration

In *The Book on Adler*, which was published only after Kierkegaard's death, Søren claims that "religiousness lies in subjectivity, in inwardness, in being deeply moved, in being jolted, in the qualitative pressure on the spring of subjectivity" (KW 24, 104). "Just as it is an excellence to be truly in love, truly *enthusiastic* [my emphasis], so it is also an excellence, in the religious sense, to be shaken. . . . And this emotion is in turn the true working capital and the true wealth" (KW 24, 108). Kierkegaard[67] spells out the idea at greater length:

> To be shaken (somewhat in the sense in which one speaks of shaking someone in order to awaken him) is the more universal basis of all religiousness; being shaken, being deeply moved, and subjectivity's coming into existence in the inwardness of emotion, are shared by the pious pagan [i.e., Socrates] and the pious Jew [e.g., Philo of Alexandria] in common with a Christian. (KW 24, 112–113)

On the same page (113), he continues to say that Christianity's distinct conceptual categories do, and ought to, shape any distinctly Christian experience. (A Christian, for Kierkegaard, is not a person who votes for a xenophobic populist as President: that so-called "Christian" is a member of the awful "Christendom": see how Climacus phrases this in CUP, 45.) Yet he asserts in terms that could not be more lucid that he identifies the Christian God with Love, referring in *Works of Love* to "*love*, which is God" (WL, 265), adding that

---

[66] Rudebusch (2009, 28). Cf. Fallis (2018).

[67] Since the work was not published in Kierkegaard's lifetime, it was never assigned a pseudonym, although he considered assigning it to one when he considered (and decided against) publishing it, out of respect for Adler.

24 *The Philosophy of Søren Kierkegaard*

"God is Love" (WL, 190), and even going so far as to say that, as *middle term* between lover and beloved, "Love is God" (WL, 121).[68]

"God is Love, and therefore we can be like God only in loving" (WL, 62–63). "Love is the source of all things [trans. modified] and, in the spiritual sense, love is the deepest ground of the spiritual life" (WL, 215). These statements make it unequivocally clear that "love" remains for all time the only accurate divine name (see Pseudo-Dionysius 1987), as Kierkegaard sees it. "Love is a passion of the emotions" (WL, 112) – or, "Love is an emotional passion." Evidently this is the same point being made in the passages from *The Book on Adler* that I cited just above.

> Love's hidden life is in the innermost being, unfathomable, and then in turn is in an unfathomable connectedness with all existence. Just as the quiet lake originates deep down in hidden springs no eye has ever seen, so also does a person's love originate even more deeply in God's love [or, in God as love]. If there were no gushing spring at the base [trans. modified], *if God were not Love* [my emphasis], then there would be neither the little lake nor a human being's love. Just as the quiet lake originates darkly in the deep spring, so a human being's love originates mysteriously in God's love. (WL, 8–10)

Love is the enigmatic power at the basis of the psyche, and the deepest ground of human being. We are who we are only by virtue of being *in* love, in a relation of dependency.[69] Kierkegaard here presents what may be called a transcendental argument: love is that by virtue of which we inhabit a meaningful world. "A life without loving is not worth living" (WL, 38; see also WL, 375). Without it, everything would be confused;[70] our experience would not be organized in terms of what stands out in our consciousness as significant. In the terms of Immanuel Kant's critical philosophy, it unifies the manifold of sensory impressions; in the terms of analytic philosophy of mind, it can resolve the "frame problem" of how we focus on some things and overlook others. When we're talking about "the love that sustains all existence," we should realize that, "if for one moment, one single moment, if it were to be absent, [then] everything would be confused" (WL, 301). Love gives us focus and orientation, and – most crucially, for this Element – provides us with insight into who we are as distinct, particular human beings.

---

[68] Cf. Arnold B. Come (1999); M. Jamie Ferreira (2001). On *Kjerlighed* see also Krishek (2009, 111). Another among the very few to take Kierkegaard at his word is Jos Huls (2011). In what follows I draw upon aspects of Furtak (2005, 97–101). Cf. Furtak (2013b).

[69] In being *in* that upon which one *depends*, see O'Meara (1993, 26–27).

[70] See also Kant (1965, 645–646), A821-822/B849-850: "Persuasion cannot be subjectively distinguished from conviction. . . . The subjective sufficiency is termed *conviction*."

Kierkegaard, Socrates, and the Meaning of Life

It does not make sense to speak of the divine as if it could be encountered as an object, like "a rare, enormously large green bird with a red beak, perched on a tree on the city wall, and perhaps even whistling in a hitherto unknown-of way," as Climacus puts it (CUP, 205). When C. Stephen Evans contends that "only an objectively existing being could create a world" (Evans 1998, 158), he is mistaken. What he means to say is that God is real. But what is real is *more* than what is objective.[71] He ought to have considered that, for example, Schopenhauer's Will is precisely *not* an object, yet is capable of giving rise to the concrete world of subjects *as well as* objects that we know in our everyday lives. To characterize love as the ground of existence is to make "an ontological claim of the most fundamental kind, about the dynamic energy that founds all things."[72] Love *forms* the heart as it proceeds *from* the heart (WL, 12–13), such that only the one who loves knows who he is and what he must do (KW 4, 125). "The love-relation requires threeness: the lover, the beloved, the love – but the love is God" (WL, 121). The first person of Love is God the Father; the second person is Christ ("this is my son, my beloved"); and the third, the Holy Spirit, is *love itself.*[73] Love is the sacred force that connects us to the earthly realm in which our duty is to love the person we happen to see (WL, 154–174). By loving others, not *as* gods but *through* the God of love, we become subject to existential imperatives which are unique to each of us. To admit one's radical dependence on a God of love is not to debase oneself but to make an ennobling concession (see KW 5, 297–326). To need Love is our highest perfection, and this is how a God of love provides us with the grounding conditions of a meaningful life.[74]

When we view things with loving eyes, every aspect of the world is enriched. As the contemporary philosopher Irving Singer observes, "life cannot be meaningless to anyone who loves" (Singer 1992, 85). Love is not an objective entity but a subjective mode of comportment that enables things to manifest themselves as meaningful. "If you yourself have never been in

---

[71] This point is made throughout the phenomenological tradition, from Husserl to Zahavi. It is also articulated in striking and memorable examples by Nagel (1979, 165–180) and Nagel (1987, 8–18).

[72] Langan (1996, 311). This is present in each person "in such a way that it demands that I recognize and affirm

this same validity and dignity in every other human being" (Come 1999, 91–92).

[73] Cf. Nicholas of Cusa (1997) for the most exactly articulated formulation of this Trinitarian theology of which I am aware. This suggests that the Greek Orthodox Church was right in the theological matter that gave rise to the Great Schism, and that in the catechism the Love that proceeds "from the Father" is correct, the blasphemous innovation "and from the Son" inaccurate. Regarding what follows, see Ferreira (2001, 72): "God is not the 'middle term' by being the direct object of our love in such a way as to marginalize the beloved; God is the 'middle term' by being the center of the relationship."

[74] Cf. Frankfurt (2004, 56): insofar as love enables us to have final ends, "it is the ultimate ground of practical rationality."

love," Kierkegaard writes, "you do not know whether anyone has ever been loved in this world," for only "if you yourself have loved" have you perceived reality beyond yourself as significant, just as "the blind person cannot know color differences" (KW 17, 237). It is not a coincidental or accidental fact about us that we are loving or caring beings: rather, it is a grounding condition "of the universe of our possibilities" (Lear 2000, 33). Heidegger phrases it this way: "It is not the case that objects are first present as bare realities, as objects in some natural state, and that they then in the course of our experience receive the garb of a value-character, so they do not have to run around naked" (Heidegger 2001, 69).[75] Instead, we are *always already* rooted and grounded in love (see KW 5, 55). Human existence would be empty and vain if nothing were loved or cared about for its own sake, so we must love in order to avoid an absurd predicament. Love is the divinity that shapes our ends, to crib from Hamlet's vocabulary.

Whenever we love, then, we are divinely inspired, much in the way that Nietzsche has in mind when he pays tribute to Schopenhauer "as educator":

> What have you up to now truly loved, what attracted your soul, what dominated it while simultaneously making you happy? Place this series of revered objects before you, and perhaps their nature and their sequence will reveal to you a law, the fundamental law of your authentic self.... Your true being does not lie deeply hidden within you, but rather immeasurably high above you, or at least above what you commonly take to be your ego. (Nietzsche 1995, 174)

It may be that Kierkegaard loved his vocation as a writer more than he loved his beloved fiancée Regine Olsen. Or perhaps what set off the trumpeters of the apocalypse was something else that he admitted to her in an October 1840 letter, written during the time of their engagement: "I have now read so much by Plato on love" (KW 25, 66). For, like Plato's hero and character Socrates, Kierkegaard is a supernaturalist – that is to say, a type of idealist – for whom "meaning in life is a relationship with a spiritual realm" (Metz 2013, 79). More specifically, Kierkegaard in his own life fits Thaddeus Metz's description of someone who believes that "God's purpose [is] the sole source of invariant ethical rules" (Metz 2013, 84–85), rules pertaining to the individual *as such*.[76]

---

[75] Cf. Ratcliffe (2010, 362): mood or attunement is not "a subjective gloss, resting on top of a preunderstood objective world."

[76] Metz (2019, 32) cites Swinburne (2016, 154) on how, for the Christian, mortal life has "a cosmic significance" instead of "a significance very limited in time and space." His definition of a supernaturalist, who plainly qualifies as a non-naturalist, as "one who maintains that either God or a soul (or the pair) is central to life's meaning," can be found in Metz (2019, 6). See also

Kierkegaard, Socrates, and the Meaning of Life

Just as he accounts for love as an emotional *urge* (see Søltoft 2013), he cites this kind of motive as the source for his feeling of personal destiny. Maybe he was one of those people who, as we often hear recited, "takes himself too seriously." Then again, just how seriously *should* we take ourselves? Certainly, I dare to suggest, more seriously than we take our favorite television show.

Was Kierkegaard a religious mystic? Mystics take seriously what they experience, and Kierkegaard did this all the time. Bergson points out that "the impulse given by feeling can ... resemble obligation" and that this is especially true of "the passion of love." He adds, "anyone engaged in writing has been in a position to feel the difference between an intelligence left to itself and that which burns with the fire of an original and unique emotion."[77] And Kierkegaard does in an entry of May 19, 1838, report a feeling of "*indescribable joy*," not "a joy over this or that, but a full-bodied shout of the soul" (*Pap* II A 228 / PJ, 97), which reverberated in another conversion experience ten years later on April 19, 1848;[78] this one led him to write: "My whole being has changed" (*Pap* VIII 1 A 640 / PJ, 294–295). And he felt an urgent sense of purpose, as we will shortly see.

> Spiritually I have been a youth in the best sense of the word. Overwhelmed by God, shattered until I felt even less than a sparrow before him, I nevertheless received a positive bold confidence to dare youthfully to become involved with God. . . . Call it crazy, but in my final moment I am going to pray to God for permission to thank him once again for making me crazy this way. In fact, it is doubtful whether anyone whom God has not made crazy like this really has ever realized that he exists before God. (*Pap* X 2 A 134 / JP, 6516)

Enduring what Kierkegaard described as *terrible suffering*, he became an author. "I have struggled and suffered fearfully," trying to answer the imperative "You shall" in "an almost melancholy-manaical way" (*Pap* X 1 A 422 / JP 6416), as he writes in an entry dated June 4, 1849. Yet God has been with him during the whole process of his life, and "this is why I am so indescribably happy in the midst of all my sufferings" (*Pap* X 2 A 112 / JP, 6514), even though "being known by God makes life infinitely burdensome" (*Pap* VI A 98 / DSK, 21). Meaning in life is more important than happiness per se. Happiness tends to be over-rated,[79] whereas the importance of doing meaningful work is usually under-rated in both Kierkegaard's culture and our own.

Jerome I. Gellman, *The Fear, the Trembling, and the Fire: Kierkegaard and Hasidic Masters on the Binding of Isaac* (Washington, DC: University Press of America, 1994). In short, God did not command *anyone and everyone* to perform a sacrifice. Cf. Omri Boehm, *The Binding of Isaac* (London: Bloomsbury Academic, 2007).

[77] Bergson (1977, 39, 46).   [78] See Lowrie (1938, 400–401)

[79] Cf. Wiggins (1998, 134–136)

28 *The Philosophy of Søren Kierkegaard*

3 "So powerful an urge ...": Finding the Meaning of *Each* Life

In an 1847 journal entry, Kierkegaard writes of his literary purpose (my emphases):

> Only when I write do I feel well. Then I forget all of life's vexations, all its sufferings, then I am wrapped in thought and am happy. If I stop for a few days, right away I become ill, overwhelmed and troubled; my head feels heavy and burdened. *So powerful an urge*, so ample, so inexhaustible, one which, having subsisted day after day for five or six years, is still flowing as richly as ever, such an urge, *one would think*, must also be a vocation from God.[80]

One would think. For Kierkegaard, in order for there to be meaning *in* life, there needs to be a unifying meaning to one's life as a whole. His, above all, was defined by his task as an author, specifically – as he expresses it in *On My Work as an Author*, published in 1851 – to write in such a way as "*to make aware* of the religious" (KW 22, 12). And the criterion for this was unmistakably emotional, as he says in the related *Point of View for My Work as an Author*: "I feel a need and therefore regard it now as my duty" (KW 22, 23). "My work as an author was the prompting of an irresistible inner need" (KW 22, 24). Here he anticipates his contemporary nonconformist Henry David Thoreau (see Mooney 2012): "I hear an irresistible voice which invites me away from all that [alleged wisdom of septuagenarians]" (Thoreau 1987, 13). And what are you going to do with an irresistible inward affective impulse? Surely not resist it. As William Blake writes in the same text that I cited as an epigraph (Blake 1993, 56): "Those who restrain desire do so because theirs is weak enough to be restrained." I'm not sure that in every sense I agree with this, but we must come to terms with it in reading Kierkegaard. Just as love is an urge, the inward promptings of conscience – what Socrates called his *daimon* – are known through emotional feeling, experience that announces itself in the imperative voice. In an entry dated October 13, 1853, Kierkegaard, in surveying his literary career, writes that "the creative urge which had awakened in me was too strong to resist" (*Pap* X 5 A 146 / PJ, 559). He feels a need and therefore regards it as a duty – not at all a Kantian duty relevant to anyone and everyone but *his* duty, as the particular human being named Søren Kierkegaard. In doing so, he is referring to the notion of a divine name.

In *The Sickness unto Death*, his pseudonym "Anti-Climacus" points out that a person can "forget" his or her "name, divinely understood" (KW 19, 33–34).[81] What is it to forget our name, divinely understood? "Just as there are universal

---

[80] *Pap* VII 1 A 222 / DSK, 52. My emphasis.   [81] Cf. Krishek (2022, 7–37).

Kierkegaard, Socrates, and the Meaning of Life

qualities that are essential to being a person [any person], there are particular qualities that are essential to being the *self* that one is" (Krishek 2022, 17), where *selfhood* is "a quality that determines our identity but yet is primarily in a state of potential." Our "essence is fixed and invariable in its potential state, and is contingent and variable in its actualized state" (Krishek 2022, 52). For Kierkegaard, the former is prior to the latter. This sets the agenda for his account of how *each human being* has the potential to actualize her or his God-given potentiality in the concrete circumstances of his or her life. "God creates persons," not as impersonal vehicles of reason "but as *individual* persons" (Krishek 2022, 19). Kierkegaard was nothing if not an individual.[82] As "Anti-Climacus" affirms, "every person certainly is angular" (KW 19, 33) and must through his or her situation actualize his or her utterly unique potential. Kierkegaard introduces the category of "the single individual" (KW 14, 93n), that is, *hiin Enkelte*, and claims that none of us is exempt from being and becoming singular persons, creatures who have *Eiendommelighed* (WL, 252–253) – that is, unique or authentic individuality.[83] And this is based upon what we have loved. As Ezra Pound sings in *Canto LXXXI*, "What thou hast loved best remains, / the rest is dross" (Pound 1993, 540–541). This echoes the quotation from Nietzsche's "Schopenhauer as Educator" that I cited above, and as we shall see it fits well with Kierkegaard's way of thinking.[84]

There is *something* to be said for objectivity in all of this. But not as much as some philosophers would have us believe. For instance, "my experience of loving another person might enable me to see the value which resides in all persons" (Rudd 2012, 133), which is true enough according to Kierkegaard and to me, but he adds that among "persons who have about equally praiseworthy characteristics," I find myself bizarrely being "drawn to, attracted by, some of them, rather than others, even though I don't think they are really better persons," and regards this as somewhat unfair: "we can transcend our finitude sufficiently to *recognize* that other persons have, objectively, as much value as the ones that we do love" (*ibid.*, 133–134). It is important that I "love them as they deserve," no

---

[82] See Kaufmann (1975, 95).

[83] Arnold B. Come is especially articulate in teasing out this critical notion in *Works of Love* (Come 1995, 353–354). I have also benefited from personal communication with Deidre Green.

[84] It fits too with the spirit of Plotinus, who writes in *Enneads* V.7, "On the Question [of] whether There Are Ideas of Particulars" (trans. by A. H. Armstrong), that human beings "are not related to their form as portraits of Socrates are to their original, but their different structures must result from different forming principles," as is evidenced by the fact that "different children come from the same parents." – *Enneads* V.7.1–2. Cf. Plotinus, *Enneads* II.3.15: "We must not think of the soul as of such a kind that . . . of all things it has no nature of its own."

30   *The Philosophy of Søren Kierkegaard*

more (*ibid.*, 137). This is like saying that I "value" a kind of music that leaves me cold emotionally (see Nussbaum 2001, 278). If emotions or passions are perceptions of significance (see Furtak 2005), or embodied recognitions of meaning and value (see Furtak 2018), then whatever seems neutrally valenced to us is something we are *experiencing* as meaningless; we feel that it *is* meaningless.

According to Kierkegaard's pseudonym "Johannes *de silentio*," the conclusions of passion "are the only dependable ones – that is, the only convincing ones" (KW 6, 100). It is well and good to note that "meaning arises when subjective attraction meets objective attractiveness" (Wolf 2010, 62). After all, both I and Kierkegaard agree with Max Scheler when he speaks of an *ordo amoris* and avers that "the highest thing of which a [human being] is capable is to love things as much as possible as God loves them," which we cannot do *merely* (!) by virtue of being finite (Scheler 1973, 99), that love enables "knowledge of personal destiny," and that what we can come to know through love amounts to our "*range* of contact with the universe" (Scheler 1973, 106–107, 111). Susan Wolf, Scheler, and I tend to incline toward realism about what love reveals. However, she is way too concerned that we undertake "projects of objective value," and not get preoccupied by the project of "collecting a big ball of string" (Wolf 2010, 104), which no one ever does. Not, that is, unless it seems like a worthy enterprise to set a world record, without growing one's fingernails out to an absurd length or something like that. Kierkegaard himself did not worry about such things. His books were not books that "someone" ought to write, but ones that he had a sacred imperative from Providence, or Governance, to create. And at the basis of his passion was that supreme "passion of the emotions," namely Love. "These which present themselves to me as three, namely, the lover, the lovable, and the bond, are the absolute and most simple essence itself" (Nicholas of Cusa 1997, 268; cf. Augustine, *De Trinitate*), and by consenting to accede to where love, the hidden spring of the lake, is leading, we learn who we are and who we aspire to be. We learn what our divine name is.

The main problem with "the present age," for Kierkegaard, is that it is "without passion," devoid of passionate inspiration (KW 14, 74), "*flaring up in superficial, short-lived enthusiasm and prudentially relaxing in indolence*" (KW 14, 68). It stifles heroic ventures. We must "*give up all imaginary and exaggerated ideas about a dreamworld where the object of love should be sought and found,*" he says (WL, 161), but rather find lovable the person, the calling, that present themselves to us – to embrace and submit to our limitations. He admires Socrates as depicted in the *Phaedo* for his "passionate fidelity" to his mission, "as expressed in the conduct of his life" (Howland 2006, 44; again, see CUP,

Kierkegaard, Socrates, and the Meaning of Life

169–170). The damning fact about Adolph Peter Adler is that, after claiming to have had a revelation, he did not stick to his story but recanted – just like Don Quixote (CUP, 164), who *was* a knight errant when he lived in accordance with the belief that this is what he was. "As soon as a person is really deeply moved by something, when he is in mortal danger, when the extraordinary appears before him, when he stands impassioned with his future fate in his hands, there is immediately an either/or" (KW 24, 48n). Magister Adler "does not understand himself in what has happened to him," for "he has not even made up his mind about what is to be understood by a revelation" and whether or not he himself had one (KW 24, 115). Kierkegaard, by contrast, kept reaffirming his account of himself, even amidst its endless visions and revisions. His own loving subjectivity was centered on a passion for writing, as we have seen; it is hard to imagine what he would be like without this life-defining passion. That is one reason why it is difficult to imagine how to interpret his May 17, 1843, remark that "if I had faith, I would have stayed with Regine" (*Pap* IV A 107 / PJ, 160–161). Stayed with her, and still written *The Sickness unto Death?*

Becoming who one is involves a curious mixture of inner enthusiasm and external accident, since in Krishek's terms we are neither more eternal than temporal nor more temporal than eternal but a "synthesis" of these dual factors (KW 19, 13). We are composed like works of art, but we are not the artist – at most, we are coauthors of our biography (cf. KW 15, 198–199). Nietzsche, that champion of the will, acknowledges the passivity of inspiration when he states in *Beyond Good and Evil* that "a thought comes when 'it' wishes, and not when 'I' wish" (1997a, § 17). He expresses gratitude for his entire life, says that "the fortunateness of my existence, its uniqueness perhaps, lies in its fatality," and adds that "*amor fati* is my innermost nature."[85] Although any notion of a supernatural capacity would be regarded by Nietzsche as most likely "a kind of philosophical fantasy" (Pippin 2010, 3), when it comes to how the divine inhabits the finite, he and Kierkegaard are very much on the same page. And so is Proust – whose narrator echoes Emerson when, accounting for how the heart has something like *reasons of its own*, he notes that for issues "close to one's heart," our "beliefs are entirely determined by whim."[86] Here is a Kierkegaardian passage from 1846:

> A conviction [*Overbeviisning*] is called a conviction because it is *over* and *above* proof [*Beviisning*]. Proof is given for a mathematical proposition in

---

[85] Friedrich Nietzsche, *Ecce Homo* (1979a, 7–8, 94). Cf. Leiter (1998, 222).

[86] Antoine Panaioti, "Proust and Nietzsche on Self-Fashioning" (2023, 424).

32 *The Philosophy of Søren Kierkegaard*

such a way that no disproof is conceivable. For that reason there can be no conviction with respect to mathematics.[87] But as far as every existential proposition is concerned, for every proof there is some disproof, there are a *pro* and a *contra* [a reference to Aristotle's logic]. The man of conviction is not ignorant of this; he knows well enough what doubt is able to say … but nevertheless, or, more correctly, for that very reason, he is a man of conviction, because he has made a resolution. (*Pap* VII 1 A 215 / JP, 2296)

"The idea for which he was willing to live and die was in fact the production of dazzling literary work," as one biographer concludes (Garff 2005, 59). He refers to the following passage dated August 1, 1835, written during a stay at the Gilleleje Inn on the Zealand coast north of Copenhagen. I am not the first reader of Kierkegaard to cite this.

> Just as a child takes time to learn to distinguish itself from objects, … what I really need is to be clear about *what I am to do*, not what I must know, except in the way knowledge must precede all action. It is a question of understanding my own destiny, of seeing what the Deity really wants *me* to do; the thing is to find a truth which is truth *for me*, to find *the idea for which I am willing to live and die*. And what use would it be in this respect if I were to discover a so-called objective truth, [to] construct a world which, again, I myself did not inhabit but merely held up for others to see? … What use would it be if truth were to stand there before me, cold and naked, not caring whether I acknowledged it or not, inducing an anxious shiver rather than trusting devotion? (AA:12 / KJN 1, 19)

As he proceeds to write in this nugget-filled journal entry, he needs to ground his orientation in "something which is bound up with the deepest roots of my existence, through which I have, as it were, grown into the divine, clinging fast to it even if the whole world were to fall apart. *This, you see, is what I need, and this is what I strive for*. … It is this inward action of the human, this God-side of man, that matters" (AA:12 / KJN 1, 20–21). And, doubtless thinking of Socrates, he says that "the genuine philosopher is in the highest degree subjective" (AA:12 / KJN 1, 20); further: "How near is man to madness in any case despite all his knowledge? What is truth other than living for an idea? Everything must in the final analysis be based on a postulate. But the moment when it no longer stands outside him but he lives in it, only then, for him, does it cease to be a postulate" (AA:12 / KJN 1, 21). And, finally, "one must first learn to know oneself before knowing anything else (*gnothi seauton*). Only when the

---

[87] Only phenomena so poor in existential relevance can be so rich in certainty, as Kant realized. Cf. Marion (2007, 9): in speaking of love, "I will not be able to hide myself behind the *I* of philosophers, that *I* who is supposed to be universal, a disengaged spectator. … In contrast, I am going to speak of that which affects each of us as such."

Kierkegaard, Socrates, and the Meaning of Life   33

person has inwardly understood *himself*, and then sees the way forward on his path, does his life acquire repose and meaning" (AA:12 / KJN 1, 22).

To highlight some aspects of this: self-knowledge, not in the sense of *how do indexical pronouns refer*[88] but as a kind of emotional knowing of my purpose, to which I can devote myself, a *relevant* truth that does not remain coldly indifferent to me but a subjective conviction, is a condition for living meaningfully and feeling grounded. Moreover, the source of subjective conviction is *divine* and may be described as a form of holy madness, of *theia mania* (see Plato, *Phaedrus*).

What answer did Kierkegaard receive on his pilgrimage to Gilleleje? Maybe nothing too convincing – not yet, at least. But he must have had an inkling of the subjective and existential truth that he sought, because two and a half years later when he falls in love with Regine he asks himself whether *this* love, rather than his literary mission, ought to direct his life.

> Oh, can I really believe what the poets say: that when a man sees the beloved object for the first time he believes he has seen her long before, that all love, as all knowledge, is recollection, that love in the single individual also has its prophecies, its types, its myths, its Old Testament? . . . You blind God of love! You who see in secret, will you make it known to me? Am I to find here in this world what I seek, am I to experience the conclusion of all my life's eccentric premises, am I to conclude you in my embrace – or: *Do the orders say: march on?* (*Pap* II A 347 / PJ, 100–101)

As he writes in *Works of Love*, "what is the eternal foundation must also be the foundation of every expression of the particular" (WL, 141). Love as divine source manifests itself in forming the heart as it flows from the heart (WL, 12–13) into the concrete passions that define the meaning of life for each of us. Knowing oneself means wholeheartedly loving what one loves.

4 "The true life of the individual": Kierkegaardian *Amor Fati*

In his novel *In Search of Lost Time*, Marcel Proust's narrator develops what to my ears sounds like a Kierkegaardian (or Nietzschean) conception of "our true life," that is, "reality as we have felt it to be." This determines "the qualitative difference, the uniqueness of the fashion in which the world appears to each one of us."[89] Discovering *that* requires "the courage of our emotions."[90] This

---

[88] John Perry's example of self-knowledge is how I can know that the person at the grocery store leaving a trail of sugar is I myself (1994, 167). His paper features the amusing misprint of "trial" for "trail" in its opening sentence.

[89] *Remembrance of Things Past: Volume Three* (1982, 931, 915).

[90] *Remembrance of Things Past: Volume Three* (1982, 932).

34 *The Philosophy of Søren Kierkegaard*

narrator even appropriates the notion of "subjective truth."[91] He is speaking not about the self as an inner entity that must only be released from its box in order to spring to life fully formed. Our distinct individuality is based in our native temperament and is acquired through our romantic encounter with the world. Proust's narrator points out that it is challenging to understand who we are, saying that he was "mistaken in thinking that I could see clearly into my own heart."[92] Hence the requisite courage of one's emotions. What is at issue in grasping our idiosyncratic personal identity, our destiny, is nothing less than the meaning of life. This would constitute "the highest truth there is for someone *existing*," in the words of Kierkegaard's pseudonym in the *Postscript* (CUP, 171). In the midst of existence and its uncertainty, the Dane himself writes, "one must acknowledge that in the final analysis there is no theory" (SKS 22, 396 / KJN 6, 401). But we are not mere bundles of external coincidences, things that happen to us – *contra* Rorty – nor are we only our inborn genetic code.[93] We are both shaped by contingencies of environment and biography *and* utterly singular in our innate God-given uniqueness. Krishek captures this concisely when she says that "we are neither more eternal than temporal nor more temporal than eternal" (Krishek 2022, 55). Rather, we are a synthesis of the two. On a loose paper dated July 4, 1840, Kierkegaard writes one of the most important and memorable passages in all of his unpublished works:

> The historical is namely the unity of the metaphysical and the accidental. It is the metaphysical insofar as this is the eternal bond of existence without which the phenomenological would disintegrate; it is the accidental insofar as there is in every event a possibility that it could take place in infinitely many other ways; seen from the divine standpoint, the unity of this is *Providence*; from the human standpoint, *the historical.* . . . This unity of the metaphysical and the accidental is already present in self-consciousness, which is the point of departure for the personality. I become at the same time conscious of myself in my eternal validity, in my, so to speak, divine necessity, and in my accidental finitude (that I am this particular being, born in this country, at this time, under the influence of all these varied circumstances). And this latter aspect is not to be overlooked and not rejected, but *the true life of the individual is its apotheosis* [my emphasis], which does not consist in the empty content-less I stealing away, as it were, out of this finitude in order to be volatilized and evaporated in its emigration to heaven, but that *the divine dwells within and finds itself in the finite* [my emphasis]. (*Papir* 264 / KJN, 11:1, 236)

---

[91] *Remembrance of Things Past: Volume Three* (1982, 355).

[92] *Remembrance of Things Past: Volume Three* (1982, 426).

[93] Quoting Freud's essay on Leonardo da Vinci (*Standard Edition* XI, 137) in support of this claim, Rorty praises Freud for helping to "de-divinize the self by tracking conscience home to its origin in the contingencies of our upbringing." – Richard Rorty (1989, 30–31). The Kierkegaardian innate self is most decidedly a "divinized" self.

Kierkegaard, Socrates, and the Meaning of Life   35

Recounting how to find the meaning of one's ownmost existence, Kierkegaard claims both that we are shaped by "divine necessity" *and* that the "true life of the individual" is nothing less than the "apotheosis" of our finitude, our contingency. We might even speak of him turning every "thus it was" into "thus God willed it."

Proust's narrator does manage to look back at what becomes the history of a vocation – and this, in the future perfect tense, is the author he *will have become*.[94] And Kierkegaard, in his personal unpublished notebooks, increasingly over the years looked retrospectively at all he had become and all he had done as the invisible history of his own calling as a religious writer. This relentless, obsessive, manic (see Furtak 2022, 103–108) quest played itself out in multiplying drafts, each one always subject to further revision, with his own melancholy or mental heaviness (*Tungsind*), his father's sins, and his broken engagement with Regine Olsen always figuring into leading roles in the "play" (see Andreas-Salomé 1995, xi) that was not a fiction but rather his enacted, finite life. In Lou Salomé's words again, human beings are "forced to come to terms with that by which we are merely carried" (Andreas-Salomé 1995, 17).[95] Recall Bergson's remarks about being carried along on a wave of inspiration. We will view the history of Kierkegaard's frustrating and yet fulfilling love affair with the world in greater depth soon. For now, let me mention that Kierkegaard's description pertains to each human being, not only those who are as intensely "possessed" as he was. For we are, every one of us, created in God's image and capable of *enthusiasm* in the Greek sense – in other words, of being divinely inspired from within.

Emerson, that instigator of Nietzsche (see Stack, 1992), declares in "Self-Reliance" that he will "shun father and mother and wife and brother when my genius calls me. I would write on the lintels of the door-post, *Whim.* I hope it is somewhat better than whim at last, but we cannot spend the day in explanation."[96] He refers to the Passover tradition of anointing the doorposts with the blood of a sacrificed lamb to protect those inside;[97] that is, Emerson

---

[94] See Ricoeur, who describes "the sudden illumination that retrospectively transforms the entire narrative into the invisible history of a vocation" – *Time and Narrative, Volume Two* (1985, 131–132).

[95] See Andreas-Salomé (1995, 13): "Elevated by the intoxication of love, I was able . . . to come to terms with reality." Socrates calls it a kind of "divine madness" in the *Phaedrus* and a "divine power" of mad inspiration in Plato, *Ion* 533d-534b. On the *Ion* see Beversluis (2000, 75–93). On *Phaedrus* 244a-245b, see Nussbaum (1986, 213–222) and Nussbaum (1991). On Lou Salomé and Friedrich Nietzsche, see Young (2010, 339–356).

[96] Emerson (1993, 26–27).

[97] See G. E. M. Anscombe, *On Transubstantiation*, 5. Cf. Cavell, "An Emerson Mood" (1992, 155): "If we could know in advance of . . . whim that it will truly prove to have been our genius

claims that in order to obey his *genius* – we might say, his *daimon* – he will enshrine the sanctity of even whimsical inspiration. "A foolish consistency is the hobgoblin of little minds" (Emerson 1993, 30). For Kierkegaard, though the search for personal unity and integrity means more,[98] the enshrinement of one's *daimon* as sacred authority is just as strong as it is in Socrates' defense at his trial.

Nietzsche's term for a love that would affirm what Kierkegaard calls the eternal and the contingent is *amor fati*, the love of fate (an idea with ancient Greek origins, as he knows).

> I want to learn more and more how to see what is necessary in things as what is beautiful in them – thus I will be one of those who make things beautiful. *Amor fati:* let that be my love from now on! . . . Let *looking away* be my only negation! And, all in all and on the whole: some day I want only to be a Yes-sayer![99]

This echoes a couple of sentences by Kierkegaard: "What one sees depends upon how one sees; all observation is not just a receiving, a discovering, but also a bringing forth, and insofar as it is that, how the observer is constituted is indeed decisive. When one person sees one thing and another sees something else in the same thing, then the one discovers what the other conceals" (KW 5, 59). It also resonates with his claim that love "makes a person blind in the deepest and noblest and most blessed sense of the word, so that he blindly loves every human being as the lover loves the beloved" (WL, 69), and with his discussion of what it means to love the person we see, as well as what it means for love to believe all things.

Viewing *what is* as *what ought to be* qualifies as creating beauty. Such affirmation of existence is the antidote to nihilism and a necessary condition of living meaningfully.[100] One early formulation of Nietzsche's defines it this way: "His holy will be done! All he gives I will joyfully accept: happiness and

---

 that has called us, then the gate to salvation would not be strait; there would be little need for faith, and little to write about."

[98] Cf. George Connell, *To Be One Thing: Personal Unity in Kierkegaard's Thought* (Macon, GA: Mercer University Press, 1985), esp. 1–37. He alludes to the discourse "Purity of Heart is to Will One Thing" (KW 15, 3–154).

[99] This is from *The Gay Science* § 276 in Friedrich Nietzsche (2001a, 157). Remarkably similar, on making things beautiful, is a passage from *Walden*: "It is something to be able to paint a particular picture, or to carve a statue, and so to make a few objects beautiful; but it is far more glorious to carve and paint the very atmosphere and medium through which we look, which morally we can do. To affect the quality of the day, that is the highest of arts" – Thoreau (1987, 60).

[100] As one Nietzschean asks, "Is it a matter of beaming versus shrugging? And is that enough? To affirm life in all its richness, which includes on the comprehensive reading in all its poverty, . . . involves taking up an attitude which welcomes whatever it finds" – Tanner (2000, 79).

Kierkegaard, Socrates, and the Meaning of Life 37

unhappiness, poverty and wealth [this sounds like a wedding vow for one's love of existence], and boldly look even death in the face."[101] Nothing could pose quite so difficult a test for affirming life as painful suffering that "we do not want but which befalls us unbidden," without our having wished for it.[102] The article of faith that *amor fati* involves is cast in the future perfect tense again: namely, that what has transpired in one's life *will have made sense*, if only from a divine vantage point. Kierkegaard put into practice what Nietzsche would later preach: as György Lukács puts it, the great Dane lived "in such a way that every moment of his life became rounded into the grand gesture" (1971, 41). Did not his beloved mother's death precipitate a fruitful spiritual crisis? Wasn't it a meaningful contingency when he went to speak with Jakob Peter Mynster and Mynster was not home? Didn't it mean something hugely significant when Regine nodded to him at church? Had not the resentful lampooning of Kierkegaard in *The Corsair* (see KW 13) prompted the second stage of his work as an author? And so on.

"It is quite true what philosophy says: that life must be understood backwards. But then one forgets the other principle: that it must be lived forwards," which means "that temporal life can never properly be understood" by one who exists in time and is thus always unfinished (*Pap* IV A 164 / PJ, 161). Temporal existence never becomes fully intelligible. We pay for what Samuel Beckett, following Schopenhauer, calls "the sin of having been born" through our "incurable optimism" which leads us to affirm all of life, hoping that it ends up making sense somehow.[103] The truthfulness of a loving subjectivity cannot be endorsed unless it accepts everything we *would have* wanted to be otherwise.[104] What we have loved best remains.

Edward Mooney, to whom this little Element is dedicated, writes that "Beethoven's late quartets ... insert persistent not just passing dissonance that nevertheless does not devastate the sense of key completely" (1996, 102), and Kierkegaard's mad[105] spirituality motivated him to trace everything to God, rather than cursing the day he was born. What the unforgettable Humbert Humbert, in *Lolita*, consistently names "McFate," the governing power

---

[101] Quoted by Julian Young in *Friedrich Nietzsche: A Philosophical Biography* (2010, 18). On the same page, the biographer himself points out that "at the heart of his mature thought is the effort to rediscover ... central elements of the passionate Christian's stance to existence."

[102] Béatrice Han-Pile, "Nietzsche and the Affirmation of Life," in *The Nietzschean Mind* (2018, 454).

[103] Beckett, *Proust*, 5, 49.   [104] Cf. Furtak (2023, 135–136).

[105] Not in a bad way, but in the manner of the "divine madness" praised in Plato, *Phaedrus*; Josef Pieper (1995). See also Allan V. Horwitz and Jerome C. Wakefield (2007).

38 *The Philosophy of Søren Kierkegaard*

presiding over his American adventures (Nabokov 1997), Kierkegaard names Providence, the God of Love, or that Love which is God, the source of meaning in life. He recognizes that "we do not relate to the eternal by relating to ourselves. Any retreat from the temporal world is a retreat into the realm of self-projection, rather than a way of encountering the eternal."[106] In other words, Kierkegaard chooses to find meaning in both his privileges and his adversities, accepting profound vulnerability rather than being ruled by the "passion for eternal preservation" that "separates us from the *event* of the other, of time, of randomness, of luck, of finitude, and of love." This author continues:

> Love does not treat the finite individuality to which it attends as if it were an absolute; it sustains and affirms its finitude through a tenderness which is as singular – as random and unfair – as existence itself.[107]

Gratitude for our very being-here is gratuitous, because it is a loving trust that bears all things, hopes all things, and believes all things. Unlike his hagiographer Walter Lowrie, who entitles the final chapter of his two-volume biography "Hallelujah!,"[108] Kierkegaard regarded his own supremely meaningful existence as containing as much tragedy as triumph. Yet his God isn't an omnipotent bully or a random, indifferent flipper of coins (Ellis 2014, 119).

With his "primitive" melancholy and his "tragic" upbringing, an "authentic" love which he himself betrayed and an "involuntary" vocation that he did his best to actualize, Kierkegaard attempted heroically to perform *amor fati*.[109]

---

[106] Niels Nymann Eriksen (1998, 296).   [107] Agacinski (1998, 145–146).

[108] Lowrie (1938, 583–588).

[109] See (*Pap* IX A 70/JP, 6166) on his melancholy and upbringing, (*Pap* X 1 A 260/JP, 6385) on his having felt obligated "to demolish an authentic love." About the latter, he said many things to himself, including that maybe

"I could become happier in unhappiness *without* her than *with* her" (*Pap* X 5 A 149/ DSK, 39), and that "that I loved her, nothing is more certain" (*Pap* VIII 1 A 641/PJ, 295), along with this heartrending sequence:

"What I have lost, alas, how could you know or understand? This is a subject on which you had better stay silent – indeed how could anyone know better than I, who had made my whole extremely reflective soul into as tasteful a frame as possible for her pure, deep – and my dark – thoughts, my melancholy dreams, my scintillating hopes – and above all, all my instability; in short, all the brilliancy alongside her depth – and when I grew dizzy gazing down into her infinite affection – for nothing is as infinite as love . . . what have I lost? The only thing I loved."

"You say: she was beautiful. Oh, what do you know about that? I know, for this beauty has cost me tears – I myself brought flowers to adorn her, I would have decked her out with all the ornaments in the world – only, of course, so far as they accentuated her loveliness – and then, when she stood there in her finery, I had to leave – when her joyous, gay glance met mine, I had to leave – I went out and wept bitterly."

"She did not love my shapely nose, nor my fine eyes, nor my small feet, nor my good mind – she loved only me, and yet she didn't understand me." (*Pap* III A 147, III A 150, III A 151 / PJ, 140–141).

He did his best to accept everything, including his own mistakes and their consequences. The emotional highs and lows of a particular history of love and suffering will invariably be more intense than the experiences of someone who adopts a view from nowhere. A life of meaning is one in which we live with the ambivalent emotions that follow from unconditionally affirming our thrownness into a violently imperfect world. We embrace the metaphysically unnecessary past in its meaning for the self we have become, and we acknowledge the meanings that have oriented our existence while remaining aware of what may still be possible.[110] It is entirely fitting to allow Zarathustra to have some of the last words in this study of Kierkegaard on the meaning of life. How, he asks, could any of us endure being human, if our existence were not a perpetual opening to new dawns and horizons?

> I taught them all my creating and striving: to carry together into one what is fragment in mankind and riddle and horrid accident –
> – as poet, riddle guesser, and redeemer of chance I taught them to work on the future, and to creatively redeem everything that *was*. . . .
> This I told them was redemption.[111]

Or, as Heidegger (2011, 19) points out, the affirmation of existence "is poetizing, thinking, the godhead of the God. For Nietzsche, 'will to power' is also love." For Kierkegaard, to echo one of my epigraphs, our lives are indeed works of art, but we are not ultimately the artists in charge. Having sought an idea for which to live and die, he ended up being successful at discovering, as he expressed it in an early text, "an unshakable certainty in oneself won from all experience" (KW 1, 76). Socrates would have admired him.

Reading Kierkegaard is a vexatious but transformative experience. Therefore, you don't know what it's like until you try it. As any seasoned Kierkegaardian can attest, your time will not be wasted.

---

[110] Cf. Merleau-Ponty (2002, 488): "Each present reasserts the presence of the whole past which it supplants, and anticipates that of all that is to come."

[111] Nietzsche (2006, 158).

References

Primary Sources

Abbreviations of Kierkegaard's writings are according to this format:

CI   *The Concept of Irony*, trans. by Howard V. Hong and Edna H. Hong (Princeton, NJ: Princeton University Press, 1989).

CUP   *Concluding Unscientific Postscript*, trans. by Alastair Hannay (Cambridge: Cambridge University Press, 2009).

DSK   *The Diary of Søren Kierkegaard*, ed. by Peter Rohde, trans. by Gerta M. Andersen (New York: Carol Publishing Group, 1993).

JP   *Søren Kierkegaard's Journals and Papers*, 7 vols., ed. and trans. by Howard V. Hong and Edna H. Hong (Bloomington, IN: Indiana University Press, 1967–1978).

KJN   *Kierkegaard's Journals and Notebooks*, 11 vols., ed. by Bruce H. Kirmmse, trans. by Alastair Hannay *et al.* (Princeton, NJ: Princeton University Press, 2007–2020).

KW   *Kierkegaard's Writings*, 26 vols., ed. by Howard V. Hong and Edna H. Hong, trans. by Howard V. Hong, Edna H. Hong, Reidar Thomte, *et al.* (Princeton, NJ: Princeton University Press, 1978–2000).

Pap   *Søren Kierkegaards Papirer*, 16 vols., ed. by P. A. Heiberg, Niels Jørgen Cappelørn, Niels Thulstrup, *et al.* (Copenhagen: Gyldendal, 1909–1978).

PJ   *Papers and Journals: A Selection*, ed. and trans. by Alastair Hannay (London: Penguin Classics, 1996).

SKS   *Søren Kierkegaards Skrifter*, 28 vols., ed. by Niels Jørgen Cappelørn, Joakim Garff, Johnny Kadrup, *et al.* (Copenhagen: Gads Forlag, 1997–2013).

WL   *Works of Love*, trans. by Howard V. Hong and Edna H. Hong (Princeton, NJ: Princeton University Press, 1995).

Other Sources

Adamson, Peter (2014). *Classical Philosophy*. Oxford: Oxford University Press.

Agacinski, Sylviane (1998). "We Are Not Sublime: Kierkegaard, Abraham, and Ourselves," in *Kierkegaard: A Critical Reader*, ed. by Jonathan Rée and Jane Chamberlain, 129–150. Oxford: Blackwell.

References 41

Ahrensdorf, Peter J. (1995). *The Death of Socrates and the Life of Philosophy*. Albany, NY: SUNY Press.

Anderson, Barbara (1974). *Kierkegaard: A Fiction*. Syracuse, NY: Syracuse University Press.

Andreas-Salomé, Lou (1995). *Looking Back: Memoirs*. Trans. by Breon Mitchell. New York: Marlowe.

Andreas-Salomé, Lou (2003). *You Alone Are Real to Me*. Trans. by Angela von der Lippe. Rochester, NY: BOA Editions.

Anne, Chantal (1993). *L'Amour dans la Pensée de Søren Kierkegaard*. Paris: L'Harmattan.

Anscombe, G. Elizabeth M. (1974). *On Transubstantiation*. London: Catholic Truth Society.

Arendt, Hannah (1996). *Love and Saint Augustine*. Edited by Joanna V. Scott and Judith C. Stark. Chicago, IL: University of Chicago Press.

Aubry, Gwenaëlle (2013). "Philosophy as a Way of Life and Anti-Philosophy." In *Philosophy as a Way of Life: Ancients and Moderns*, ed. by Michael Chase, Stephen R. L. Clark, and Michael McGhee, 210–222. Oxford: Wiley-Blackwell.

Backhouse, Stephen (2016). *Kierkegaard: A Single Life*. Grand Rapids, MI: Zondervan.

Barnes, Jonathan (1987). *Early Greek Philosophy*. New York: Penguin Books.

Barrett, William (1958). *Irrational Man: A Study in Existential Philosophy*. New York: Anchor Books.

Becker, Ernest (1969). "Everyman as Pervert: An Essay on the Pathology of Normalcy." In *Angel in Armor: A Post-Freudian Perspective on the Nature of Man*, 1–38. New York: Free Press.

Beckett, Samuel (1957). *Proust*. New York: Grove Press.

Bedu-Addo, J. T. (1991). "Sense-Experience and the Argument for Recollection in Plato's *Phaedo*," *Phronesis* 36: 27–60.

Bergson, Henri (1977). *The Two Sources of Morality and Religion*. Trans. by R. Ashley Audra and Cloudesley Brereton. Notre Dame, IN: University of Notre Dame Press.

Berthold-Bond, Daniel (1991). "A Kierkegaardian Critique of Heidegger's Concept of Authenticity," *Man and World* 24 (1991): 119–142.

Beversluis, John (2000). *Cross-Examining Socrates*. Cambridge: Cambridge University Press.

Bigelow, Pat (1987). *Kierkegaard and the Problem of Writing*. Tallahassee, FL: Florida State University Press.

References

Blake, William (1993). "The Marriage of Heaven and Hell," in *The Norton Anthology of English Literature, Volume Two*, ed. by Mike H. Abrams, Robert M. Adams, Carol T. Christ, *et al.*, 53–64. New York: Norton.

Boehm, Omri (2007). *The Binding of Isaac*. London: Bloomsbury Academic.

Bollas, Christopher (1987). *The Shadow of the Object: Psychoanalysis of the Unthought Known*. New York: Columbia University Press.

Brickhouse, Thomas C. and Nicholas D. Smith (1989). *Socrates on Trial*. Princeton, NJ: Princeton University Press.

Britton, Karl (1969). *Philosophy and the Meaning of Life*. London: Cambridge University Press.

Buben, Adam (2016). *Meaning and Mortality in Kierkegaard and Heidegger*. Evanston, IL: Northwestern University Press.

Burger, Ronna (1984). *The Phaedo: A Platonic Labyrinth*. New Haven, CT: Yale University Press.

Camus, Albert (1991). *The Myth of Sisyphus*. Trans. by Justin O'Brien. New York: Vintage International.

Carlisle, Clare (2006). *Kierkegaard: A Guide for the Perplexed*. London: Continuum.

Carlsson, Ulrika (2021). *Kierkegaard and Philosophical Eros: Between Ironic Reflection and Aesthetic Meaning*. London: Bloomsbury Academic.

Cavell, Stanley (1995). "An Emerson Mood," in *The Senses of Walden*, 139–160. Chicago: University of Chicago Press.

Clark, Stephen R. L. (1997). "Ancient Philosophy," in *The Oxford Illustrated History of Western Philosophy*, ed. by Anthony Kenny, 1–53. Oxford: Oxford University Press.

Collins, James (1983). *The Mind of Kierkegaard*. Princeton, NJ: Princeton University Press.

Come, Arnold B. (1995). *Kierkegaard as Humanist*. Montreal: McGill-Queen's University Press.

Come, Arnold B. (1999). "Kierkegaard's Ontology of Love," in *International Kierkegaard Commentary: Works of Love*, ed. by Robert L. Perkins, 79–119. Macon, GA: Mercer University Press.

Connell, George (1985). *To Be One Thing: Personal Unity in Kierkegaard's Thought*. Macon, GA: Mercer University Press.

Cooper, John M. (2012). *Pursuits of Wisdom: Six Ways of Life in Ancient Philosophy*. Princeton, NJ: Princeton University Press.

Cornford, Francis M. (1932). *Before and after Socrates*. Cambridge: Cambridge University Press.

Daise, Benjamin (1999). *Kierkegaard's Socratic Art*. Macon, GA: Mercer University Press.

References

Damgaard, Iben (2007). "The Danger of the 'Restless Mentality of Comparison': Kierkegaard's Parables on the Lily and the Bird," *Kierkegaard Studies Yearbook* 12: 193–208.

Dilman, Ilham (1992). *Philosophy and the Philosophic Life: A Study in Plato's Phaedo*. New York: St. Martin's Press.

Diogenes Laertius (2018). *Lives of the Eminent Philosophers*. Ed. by James Miller. Trans. by Pamela Mensch. New York: Oxford University Press.

Dreyfus, Hubert, and Jane Rubin (1994). "Kierkegaard on the Nihilism of the Present Age: The Case of Commitment as Addiction," *Synthese* 98: 3–19.

Dunning, Stephen (1985). *Kierkegaard's Dialectic of Inwardness*. Princeton, NJ: Princeton University Press.

Dylan, Bob. *Lyrics: 1962–1985*. New York: Knopf.

Ebrey, David (2023). *Plato's 'Phaedo': Forms, Death, and the Philosophical Life*. Cambridge: Cambridge University Press.

Elkins, Katherine (2020). "Naming the Lyric," *Philosophy and Literature* 44: 402–417.

Ellis, Fiona (2014). *God, Value, and Nature*. Oxford: Oxford University Press.

Emerson, Ralph Waldo (1993). "Self-Reliance," in *Essays: First and Second Series*, 23–48. New York: Gramercy Books.

Emmanuel, Steven M. (1996). *Kierkegaard and the Concept of Revelation*. Albany, NY: SUNY Press.

Eriksen, Niels Nymann (1998). "Kierkegaard's Concept of Motion," *Kierkegaard Studies Yearbook* 3: 292–301.

Evans, C. Stephen (1998). "Realism and Antirealism in Kierkegaard's *Concluding Unscientific Postscript*," in *The Cambridge Companion to Kierkegaard*, ed. by Alastair Hannay and Gordon D. Marino, 154–176. Cambridge: Cambridge University Press.

Evans, Daw-Nay N. R., Jr. (2017). *Nietzsche and Classical Greek Philosophy: Beautiful and Diseased*. Lanham, MD: Lexington Books.

Fallis, Lewis (2018). *Socrates and Divine Revelation*. Rochester, NY: University of Rochester Press.

Ferreira, M. Jamie (2001). *Love's Grateful Striving*. New York: Oxford University Press.

Fichte, Johann G. (1987). *The Vocation of Man*. Translated by Peter Preuss. Indianapolis, IN: Hackett.

Frankfurt, Harry G. (2004). *The Reasons of Love*. Princeton, NJ: Princeton University Press.

Freud, Sigmund (1978). *The Standard Edition of the Complete Psychological Works*. 14 vols. Trans. by James Strachey and Anna Freud. London: Hogarth Press.

Frey, R. G. (1978). "Did Socrates Commit Suicide?" *Philosophy* 53: 106–108.

Furtak, Rick Anthony (2022). "The Experience of Possibility (and of Its Absence): The Metaphysics of Moods in Kierkegaard's Phenomenological Psychology," in *Kierkegaard's The Sickness unto Death: A Critical Guide*, ed. by Jeffrey Hanson and Sharon Krishek, 95–109. Cambridge: Cambridge University Press.

Furtak, Rick Anthony (2013a). "Kierkegaard and Greek Philosophy," in *Oxford Handbook on Kierkegaard*, ed. by George Pattison and John Lippitt, 129–149. Oxford: Oxford University Press.

Furtak, Rick Anthony (2018). *Knowing Emotions*. New York: Oxford University Press.

Furtak, Rick Anthony (2013b). "Love as a Relation to Truth: Envisioning the Person in *Works of Love*," *Kierkegaard Studies Yearbook* 18: 217–241.

Furtak, Rick Anthony (2023). *Love, Subjectivity, and Truth*. New York: Oxford University Press.

Furtak, Rick Anthony (2024). Review of Krishek (2022). *Continental Philosophy Review* 57: 135–139.

Furtak, Rick Anthony (2005). *Wisdom in Love: Kierkegaard and the Ancient Quest for Emotional Integrity*. Notre Dame, IN: University of Notre Dame Press.

Gardiner, Patrick (1988). *Kierkegaard*. Oxford: Oxford University Press.

Garff, Joakim (2005). *Søren Kierkegaard: A Biography*. Trans. by Bruce H. Kirmmse. Princeton, NJ: Princeton University Press.

Gellman, Jerome I. (1994). *The Fear, the Trembling, and the Fire: Kierkegaard and Hasidic Masters on the Binding of Isaac*. Washington, DC: University Press of America.

Gerson, Lloyd P. (2020). *Platonism and Naturalism: The Possibility of Philosophy*. Ithaca, NY: Cornell University Press.

Ghaffari, Hossein (2011). "Is Socrates a Prophet?" *Sophia* 50: 391–411.

Gordon, Jill (1999). *Turning toward Philosophy: Literary Device and Dramatic Structure in Plato's Dialogues*. University Park, PA: Pennsylvania State University Press.

Gouwens, David J. (1996). *Kierkegaard as Religious Thinker*. Cambridge: Cambridge University Press.

Green, Deidre Nicole (2019). "To Be(come) Love Itself: Charity as Acquired Originality." *Kierkegaard Studies Yearbook* 24: 217–240.

Green, Ronald M. (1992). *Kierkegaard and Kant: The Hidden Debt*. Albany, NY: SUNY Press.

Grøn, Arne (2008). *The Concept of Anxiety in Søren Kierkegaard*. Trans. by Jeanettte B. L. Knox. Macon, GA: Mercer University Press.

References 45

Grube, George M. A. (1958). *Plato's Thought*. Boston: Beacon Press.

Guthrie, William K. C. (1971). *Socrates*. Cambridge: Cambridge University Press.

Hadot, Pierre (1995). *Philosophy as a Way of Life*. Trans. by Michael Chase. Oxford: Blackwell.

Hadot, Pierre (1998). *The Inner Citadel*. Trans. by Michael Chase. Cambridge, MA: Harvard University Press.

Hadot, Pierre (2002). *What Is Ancient Philosophy?* Trans. by Michael Chase. Cambridge, MA: Harvard University Press.

Hall, Harrison (1984). "Love and Death: Kierkegaard and Heidegger on Authentic and Inauthentic Human Existence," *Inquiry* 27: 179–197.

Hamlyn, David W. (1990). *The Penguin History of Western Philosophy*. New York: Penguin Books.

Hannay, Alastair (2001). *Kierkegaard: A Biography*. Cambridge: Cambridge University Press.

Hannay, Alastair (2020). *Kierkegaard: Existence and Identity in a Post-Secular World*. London: Bloomsbury

Hannay, Alastair (2018). *Søren Kierkegaard*. London: Reaktion Books.

Han-Pile, Béatrice (2018). "Nietzsche and the Affirmation of Life," in *The Nietzschean Mind*, ed. by Paul Katsafanas, 448–467. London: Routledge.

Hanson, Jeffrey (2017). *Kierkegaard and the Life of Faith*. Bloomington, IN: Indiana University Press.

Harold, James A. (2004). *An Introduction to the Love of Wisdom*. Lanham, MD: University Press of America.

Hartle, Ann (1986). *Death and the Disinterested Spectator: An Inquiry into the Nature of Philosophy*. Albany, NY: SUNY Press.

Heidegger, Martin (2008). *Basic Concepts of Ancient Philosophy*. Trans. by Richard Rojcewicz. Bloomington, IN: Indiana University Press.

Heidegger, Martin (1996). *Being and Time*. Trans. by Joan Stambaugh. Albany, NY: SUNY Press.

Heidegger, Martin (2015). *The Beginning of Western Philosophy*. Trans. by Richard Rojcewicz. Bloomington, IN: Indiana University Press.

Heidegger, Martin (2011). *Introduction to Philosophy – Thinking and Poetizing*. Trans. by Phillip Jacques Braunstein. Bloomington, IN: Indiana University Press.

Heidegger, Martin (2001). *Phenomenological Interpretations of Aristotle*. Trans. by Richard Rojcewicz. Bloomington, IN: Indiana University Press.

Helms, Eleanor (2021). "Hope and the Chaos of Imagination in Kant and Kierkegaard," *History of European Ideas*, 47: 456–469.

References

Horky, Phillip Sidney (2013). *Plato and Pythagoreanism*. Oxford: Oxford University Press.

Horowitz, Allan V., and Jerome C. Wakefield (2007). *The Loss of Sadness: How Psychiatry Transformed Normal Sorrow into Depressive Disorder*. Oxford: Oxford University Press.

Howland, Jacob (2006). *Kierkegaard and Socrates*. Cambridge: Cambridge University Press.

Hughes, Carl S. (2014). *Kierkegaard and the Staging of Desire*. New York: Fordham University Press.

Huls, Jos (2011). "Love Founded in God," *HTS Theological Studies*, 67.3: 1–10.

Husserl, Edmund (1970). *The Crisis of European Sciences and Transcendental Phenomenology*. Trans. by David Carr. Evanston, IL: Northwestern University Press.

Irwin, Terence (1989). *Classical Thought*. New York: Oxford University Press.

James, William (1984). "The Will to Believe," in *The Essential Writings*, ed. by Bruce W. Wilshire, 309–325. Albany, NY: SUNY Press.

Jollimore, Troy (2011). *Love's Vision*. Princeton, NJ: Princeton University Press.

Kanayama, Yahei (2000). "The Methodology of the Second Voyage and the Proof of the Soul's Indestructibility in Plato's *Phaedo*," *Oxford Studies in Ancient Philosophy* 18: 41–100.

Kant, Immanuel (1965). *Critique of Pure Reason*. Trans. by Norman Kemp Smith. New York: St. Martin's Press.

Kaufmann, Walter (1975). *Existentialism from Dostoevsky* [sic] *to Sartre*. New York: New American Library.

Kingsley, Peter (1995). *Ancient Philosophy, Mystery, and Magic*. Oxford: Clarendon Press.

Kingsley, Peter (2020). *Reality*. London: Catafalque Press.

Kirk, Stephen Kirk, Raven, John Earle, and Schofield, Malcolm (1983). *The Presocratic Philosophers*. 2nd ed. Cambridge: Cambridge University Press.

Krishek, Sharon (2009). *Kierkegaard on Faith and Love*. Cambridge: Cambridge University Press.

Krishek, Sharon (2022). *Lovers in Essence: A Kierkegaardian Defense of Romantic Love*. New York: Oxford University Press.

Landy, Joshua (2004). *Philosophy as Fiction*. Oxford: Oxford University Press.

Langan, Thomas (1996). *Being and Truth*. Columbia, MO: University of Missouri Press.

Lear, Jonathan (2000). *Happiness, Death, and the Remainder of Life*. Cambridge, MA: Harvard University Press.

References

47

Lefevre, Perry D. (1956). *The Prayers of Kierkegaard*. Chicago, IL: University of Chicago Press.

Leiter, Brian (1998). "The Paradox of Fatalism and Self-Creation in Nietzsche," in *Willing and Nothingness: Schopenhauer as Nietzsche's Educator*, ed. by Christopher Janaway, 217–257. Oxford: Clarendon Press.

Lippitt, John (2013). *Kierkegaard and the Problem of Self-Love*. Cambridge: Cambridge University Press.

Lippitt, John (2016). *The Routledge Guidebook to Kierkegaard's Fear and Trembling*. 2nd ed. London: Routledge.

Lowrie, Walter (1938). *Kierkegaard*. 2 vols. London: Oxford University Press.

Lukács, György (1971). *Soul and Form*. Trans. by Anna Bostock. New York: Columbia University Press.

Mackey, Louis (1972). *Kierkegaard: A Kind of Poet*. Philadelphia, PA: University of Pennsylvania Press.

Mackey, Louis (1986). *Points of View*. Talahassee, FL: Florida State University Press.

Magee, Bryan (2001). *The Story of Philosophy*. New York: Dorling Kindersley.

Marino, Gordon (2001). *Kierkegaard in the Present Age*. Milwaukee, WI: Marquette University Press.

Marion, Jean-Luc (2002). *Prolegomena to Charity*. Trans. by Stephen E. Lewis. New York: Fordham University Press.

Marion, Jean-Luc (1998). *Reduction and Givenness*. Trans. by Thomas A. Carlson. Evanston, IL: Northwestern University Press.

Marion, Jean-Luc (2007). *The Erotic Phenomenon*. Trans. by Stephen E. Lewis. Chicago, IL: University of Chicago Press.

Maughan-Brown, Frances, and Rick Anthony Furtak (2025). *Kierkegaard and the Poetry of the Gospel*. London: Bloomsbury Academic.

McCarthy, Vincent A. (2015). *Kierkegaard as Psychologist*. Evanston, IL: Northwestern University Press.

McPherran, Mark (1996). *The Religion of Socrates*. University Park, PA: Pennsylvania State University Press.

Mehl, Peter J. (2005). *Thinking through Kierkegaard: Existential Identity in a Pluralistic World*. Urbana, IL: University of Illinois Press.

Merleau-Ponty, Maurice (2002). *Phenomenology of Perception*. Trans. by Colin Smith. London: Routledge.

Metz, Thaddeus (2019). *God, Soul and the Meaning of Life*. Cambridge: Cambridge University Press.

Metz, Thaddeus (2013). *Meaning in Life: An Analytic Study*. Oxford: Oxford University Press.

48 *References*

Miles, Thomas P. (2013). *Kierkegaard and Nietzsche on the Best Way of Life*. Basingstoke: Palgrave Macmillan.

Miyawaki, Edison (2000). "Emotional Man," *Yale Review* 88.4: 143–157.

Mooney, Edward F. (1996). *Selves in Discord and Resolve*. London: Routledge.

Mooney, Edward F. (2007). *On Søren Kierkegaard*. Burlington, VT: Ashgate.

Mooney, Edward F. (2012). "Wonder and Affliction," in *Thoreau's Importance for Philosophy*, ed. by Rick Anthony Furtak, Jonathan Ellsworth, and James D. Reid, 159–184. New York: Fordham University Press.

Muench, Paul (2010a). "*Apology*: Kierkegaard's Socratic Point of View." In *Kierkegaard and the Greek World, Tome I: Socrates and Plato*, ed. by Jon Stewart and Katalin Nun, 3–25. Burlington, VT: Ashgate.

Muench, Paul (2010b). "Kierkegaard's Socratic Pseudonym." In *Kierkegaard's Concluding Unscientific Postscript: A Critical Guide*, ed. by Rick Anthony Furtak, 25–44. Cambridge: Cambridge University Press.

Mullen, John Douglas (1995). *Kierkegaard's Philosophy: Self-Deception and Cowardice in the Present Age*. Lanham, MD: University Press of America.

Murchland, Bernard (2008). *The Arrow that Flies by Day: Existential Images of the Human Condition from Socrates to Hannah Arendt*. Lanham, MD: University Press of America.

Nabokov, Vladimir (1997). *Lolita*. New York: Vintage International.

Nagel, Thomas (1979). *Mortal Questions*. Cambridge: Cambridge University Press.

Nagel, Thomas (1986). *The View from Nowhere*. Oxford: Oxford University Press.

Nagel, Thomas (1987). *What Does It All Mean?* Oxford: Oxford University Press.

Nails, Debra (2009). "The Trial and Death of Socrates," in *A Companion to Greek and Roman Political Thought*, ed. by Ryan K. Balot, 323–338. Oxford: Blackwell.

Nehamas, Alexander (1998). *The Art of Living*. Los Angeles, CA: University of California Press.

Nehamas, Alexander (1985). *Nietzsche: Life as Literature*. Cambridge, MA: Harvard University Press.

Nehamas, Alexander (2007). *Only a Promise of Happiness*. Princeton, NJ: Princeton University Press.

Nehamas, Alexander (1975). "Plato on the Imperfection of the Sensible World," *American Philosophical Quarterly* 12: 105–117.

Neto, José (1995). *The Christianization of Pyrrhonism: Skepticism and Faith in Pascal, Kierkegaard, and Shestov*. Dordrecht: Kluwer.

References 49

Neu, Jerome (1996). "*Odi et Amo*: On Hating the Ones We Love." In *Freud and the Passions*, ed. by John O'Neill, 53–72. University Park, PA: Pennsylvania State University Press.

Nicholas of Cusa (1997). "On the Vision of God," in *Selected Spiritual Writings*, trans. by H. Lawrence Bond, 233–289. New York: Paulist Press.

Nietzsche, Friedrich (1997a). *Beyond Good and Evil*. Trans. by Helen Zimmern. Mineola, NY: Dover.

Nietzsche, Friedrich (1979a). *Ecce Homo: How One Becomes what One Is*. Trans. by R. J. Hollingdale. London: Penguin Classics.

Nietzsche, Friedrich (1979b). *Philosophy and Truth*. Trans. by Daniel Breazeale. Amherst, NY: Humanity Books.

Nietzsche, Friedrich (1962). *Philosophy in the Tragic Age of the Greeks*. Trans. by Marianne Cowan. Washington, DC: Regnery.

Nietzsche, Friedrich (2001a). *The Gay Science*. Ed. by Bernard Williams. Trans. by Josefine Nauckhoff and Adrian Del Caro. Cambridge: Cambridge University Press.

Nietzsche, Friedrich (2001b). *The Pre-Platonic Philosophers*. Trans. by Greg Whitlock. Urbana, IL: University of Illinois Press.

Nietzsche, Friedrich (1995). "Schopenhauer as Educator," in *Unfashionable Observations*, trans. by Richard T. Gray, 169–255. Stanford, CA: Stanford University Press.

Nietzsche, Friedrich (2006). *Thus Spoke Zarathustra*. Trans. by Adrian Del Caro. Cambridge: Cambridge University Press.

Nietzsche, Friedrich (1997b). *Twilight of the Idols*. Trans. by Richard Polt. Indianapolis, IN: Hackett.

Nightingale, Andrea (2021). *Philosophy and Religion in Plato's Dialogues*. Cambridge: Cambridge University Press.

Nordentift, Kresten (1972). *Kierkegaard's Psychology*. Trans. by Bruce H. Kirmmse. Pittsburgh, PA: Duquesne University Press.

Nussbaum, Martha C. (1980). "Aristophanes and Socrates on Learning Practical Wisdom," *Yale Classical Studies* 26: 43–97.

Nussbaum, Martha C. (1985). "Commentary on Edmunds," *Boston Area Colloquium in Ancient Philosophy* 1: 231–240.

Nussbaum, Martha C. (1995). *Poetic Justice: The Literary Imagination and Public Life*. Boston, MA: Beacon Press.

Nussbaum, Martha C. (1986). *The Fragility of Goodness: Luck and Ethics in Greek Tragedy and Philosophy*. Cambridge: Cambridge University Press.

Nussbaum, Martha C. (1994). *The Therapy of Desire*. Princeton, NJ: Princeton University Press.

50 References

Nussbaum, Martha C. (1991). "The Transfigurations of Intoxication: Nietzsche, Schopenhauer, and Dionysus," *Arion: A Journal of Humanities and the Classics* 1.2: 75–111.

Nussbaum, Martha C. (2001). *Upheavals of Thought: The Intelligence of Emotions*. Cambridge: Cambridge University Press.

O'Meara, Dominic J. (1993). *Plotinus*. Oxford: Clarendon Press.

Panaioti, Antoine (2023). "Proust and Nietzsche on Self-Fashioning," in *The Proustian Mind*, ed. by Anna Elsner and Thomas Stern, 414–430. London: Routledge.

Pattison, George (2011). *God and Being*. Oxford: Oxford University Press.

Pattison, George (1992). *Kierkegaard: The Aesthetic and the Religious*. New York: St. Martin's Press.

Pattison, George (2005). *The Philosophy of Kierkegaard*. Montreal: McGill-Queens University Press.

Peperzak, Adrian T. (2003). *The Quest for Meaning*. New York: Fordham University Press.

Perry, John (1994). "The Problem of the Essential Indexical," in *Self-Knowledge*, ed. by Quassim Cassam, 167–183. Oxford: Oxford University Press.

Peterson, Sandra (2011). *Socrates and Philosophy in the Dialogues of Plato*. Cambridge: Cambridge University Press.

Pieper, Josef (1995). *"Divine Madness": Plato's Case against Secular Humanism*. Trans. by Lothar Krauth. San Francisco, CA: Ignatius Press.

Pippin, Robert B. (2010). *Nietzsche, Psychology, and First Philosophy*. Chicago, IL: University of Chicago Press.

Plato (1981). *Five Dialogues*. Trans. by G. M. A. Grube. Indianapolis, IN: Hackett.

Plotinus (1966–1988). *Enneads*. 7 vols. Trans. by A. H. Armstrong. Cambridge, MA: Harvard University Press.

Podmore, Simon D. (2011). *Kierkegaard and the Self before God*. Bloomington, IN: Indiana University Press.

Pound, Ezra (1993). *The Cantos*. New York: New Directions.

Proust, Marcel (1982). *Remembrance of Things Past, Volume Three*. Trans. by C. K. Scott Moncrieff, Terence Kilmartin, and Andreas Mayor. New York: Vintage Books.

Pseudo-Dionysius (1987). "The Divine Names," in *Complete Works*, trans. by Colm Luibheid and Paul Rorem, 47–131. New York: Paulist Press.

Ratcliffe, Matthew (2010). "The Phenomenology of Mood and the Meaning of Life," in *The Oxford Handbook of Philosophy of Emotion*, ed. by Peter Goldie, 349–371. Oxford: Oxford University Press.

References

51

Ricken, Friedo (1991). *Philosophy of the Ancients*. Trans. by Eric Watkins. Notre Dame, IN: University of Notre Dame Press.

Ricoeur, Paul (1985). *Time and Narrative, Volume Two*. Trans. by Kathleen McLaughlin and David Pellauer. Chicago, IL: University of Chicago Press.

Rorty, Richard (1989). *Contingency, Irony, and Solidarity*. Cambridge: Cambridge University Press.

Rudebusch, George (2009). *Socrates*. Oxford: Wiley-Blackwell.

Rudd, Anthony (2012). *Self, Value, and Narrative*. Oxford: Oxford University Press.

Russell, Bertrand (1972). *The History of Western Philosophy*. New York: Simon and Schuster.

Sappho (2002). *Poems and Fragments*. Trans. by Stanley Lombardo. Indianapolis, IN: Hackett.

Scheler, Max (1973). "Ordo Amoris," in *Selected Philosophical Essays*, trans. by David R. Lachterman, 98–135. Evanston, IL: Northwestern University Press.

Schopenhauer, Arthur (1974). *Parerga and Parilipopena, Volume One*. Trans. by E. F. J. Payne. Oxford: Clarendon Press.

Singer, Irving (1992). *Meaning in Life*. New York: Free Press.

Sloterdijk, Peter (2013). *Philosophical Temperaments: From Plato to Foucault*. Trans. by Thomas Dunlap. New York: Columbia University Press.

Sløk, Johannes (1983). *Kierkegaards Univers: En Ny Guide til Geniet*. Viborg, DK: Centrum.

Söderquist, K. Brian (2010). "The Sophists: Kierkegaard's Interpretation of Socrates and the Sophists," in *Kierkegaard and the Greek World, Tome II: Aristotle and Other Greek Authors*, ed. by Jon Stewart and Katalin Nun, 165–182. Burlington, VT: Ashgate.

Søltoft, Pia (2013). "Kierkegaard and the Sheer Phenomenon of Love," *Kierkegaard Studies Yearbook* 18: 289–306.

Stack, George J. (1992). *Nietzsche and Emerson: An Elective Affinity*. Athens, OH: Ohio University Press.

Stewart, Jon B. (2020). *The Emergence of Subjectivity in the Ancient and Medieval World*. Oxford: Oxford University Press.

Stokes, Patrick (2010). *Kierkegaard's Mirrors: Interest, Self, and Moral Vision*. Basingstoke: Palgrave Macmillan.

Stokes, Patrick (2015). *The Naked Self: Kierkegaard and Personal Identity*. New York: Oxford University Press.

Strawser, Michael (1997). *Both/And: Reading Kierkegaard from Irony to Edification*. New York: Fordham University Press.

Swinburne, Richard (2016). "How God Makes Life a Lot More Meaningful," in *God and Meaning*, ed. by Joshua Seachris and Stewart Goetz, 149–163. London: Bloomsbury Academic.

Tanner, Michael (2000). *Nietzsche: A Very Short Introduction*. Oxford: Oxford University Press.

Tarnas, Richard (1991). *The Passion of the Western Mind*. New York: Ballantine Books.

Thoreau, Henry David (1987). *Walden*. Philadelphia, PA: Running Press.

Tietjen, Ruth Rebecca (2019). *Am Abgrund: Philosophische Theorie der Angst und Übung in Philosophischer Freiheit*. Paderborn: Mentis.

Tietjen, Ruth Rebecca (2021). "Religious Zeal as an Affective Phenomenon," *Phenomenology and the Cognitive Sciences* 20: 75–91.

Topping, Ryan (2007). *Two Concepts of the Soul in Plato's Phaedo*. Lanham, MD: University Press of America.

Trabattoni, Franco (2023). *From Death to Life: Key Themes in Plato's Phaedo*. Leiden: Brill.

Turnbull, Jamie (2015). "Subjectivity/Objectivity," in *Kierkegaard's Concepts, Tome V: Objectivity to Sacrifice*, ed. by Steven M. Emmanuel, William McDonald, and Jon Stewart, 1–6. Burlington, VT: Ashgate.

Vendrell Ferran, İngrid (2018). *Die Vielfalt der Erkenntnis*. Paderborn: Mentis.

Vlastos, Gregory (1991). *Socrates, Ironist and Moral Philosopher*. Ithaca, NY: Cornell University Press.

Wahl, Jean (1998). *Kierkegaard: L'Un devant l'Autre*. Paris: Hachette Littératures.

Walsh, Sylvia (1997). "Subjectivity Versus Objectivity: Kierkegaard's *Postscript* and Feminist Epistemology," in *Feminist Interpretations of Søren Kierkegaard*, ed. by Céline Léon and Sylvia Walsh, 267–285. University Park, PA: Pennsylvania State University Press.

Weiss, Roslyn (1998). *Socrates Dissatisfied*. Oxford: Oxford University Press.

Weston, Michael (1994). *Kierkegaard and Modern Continental Philosophy*. London: Routledge.

Westfall, Joseph (2007). *The Kierkegaardian Author*. Berlin: Walter de Gruyter.

Wiggins, David (1998). *Needs, Values, Truth*. Oxford: Clarendon Press.

Williams, Bernard (1973). "Deciding to Believe," in *Problems of the Self*, 136–151. Cambridge: Cambridge University Press, 1973.

Williams, Bernard (1985). *Ethics and the Limits of Philosophy*. Cambridge, MA: Harvard University Press.

Williams, Bernard (2002). *Truth and Truthfulness*. Princeton, NJ: Princeton University Press.

Wittgenstein, Ludwig (1980). *Remarks on the Philosophy of Psychology*. Trans. by G. E. M. Anscombe. 2 vols. Chicago, IL: University of Chicago Press.

Wivel, Klaus (1999). *Næsten Intet: En Jødisk Kritik af Søren Kierkegaard*. Copenhagen, DK: C. A. Reitzels Forlag.

Wolf, Susan (2010). *Meaning in Life and Why It Matters*. Princeton, NJ: Princeton University Press.

Wollheim, Richard (1999). *On the Emotions*. New Haven, CT: Yale University Press.

Woozley, A. D. (1979). *Law and Obedience: The Arguments of Plato's Crito*. Durham, NC: University of North Carolina Press.

Xenakis, Jason (1972). "Noncommittal Philosophy," *Journal of Thought* 7: 199–205.

Yonezawa, Shigeru (2004). "Socrates's Conception of Philosophy," *British Journal for the History of Philosophy* 12: 1–22.

Young, Julian (2010). *Friedrich Nietzsche: A Philosophical Biography*. Cambridge: Cambridge University Press.

Zellner, Harold (2007). "Sappho's Alleged Proof of Aesthetic Relativity," *Greek, Roman, and Byzantine Studies* 47: 257–270.

Žižek, Slavoj (2009). *The Parallax View*. Cambridge, MA: MIT Press.

Acknowledgements

Without whom I could have done nothing: Sharon Krishek, James D. Reid, Ruth Rebecca Tietjen, J. P. Rosensweig, Ulrika Carlsson, and my parents, Tom and Kay. I owe a profound debt also to Megan Altman, Shea Li Dombrowski, Nicole Hassoun, David Hildebrand, Victor Kestenbaum, Alyssa Luboff, Frances Maughan-Brown, Willow Mindich, Anne Louise Nielsen, Martha C. Nussbaum, Lucy Osler, George Pattison, Sarah Pessin, Carrie Ruiz, and Imke von Maur. As Aristotle rightly says (*EN* 1170b-1171a), friendship is both precious and rare. I also wish to thank all of the (other) Kierkegaardians and existential philosophers from whom I have learned over the past twenty years, including those from whom I have learned in the process of articulating my disagreements.

To Edward F. Mooney
and to Me (she will know what I mean)

Cambridge Elements ☰

Philosophy of Søren Kierkegaard

Rick Anthony Furtak
Colorado College

Rick Anthony Furtak is Associate Professor of Philosophy at Colorado College and past President of the Søren Kierkegaard Society (for calendar years 2013–2014). He has published two books and over twenty essays on Kierkegaard's work, including *Wisdom in Love: Kierkegaard and the Ancient Quest for Emotional Integrity* (2005) and *Kierkegaard's 'Concluding Unscientific Postscript': A Critical Guide* (2010), along with the co-edited *Kierkegaard and the Poetry of the Gospel* (2025). He has contributed to each of the *Cambridge Critical Guides* on Kierkegaard's writings, and has dozens of other philosophical and poetic publications. He is also an Editorial Board Member for *New Kierkegaard Research* and founding Book Series Co-Editor for *Bloomsbury Studies in Philosophy and Poetry*. His other recent books include *Love, Subjectivity, and Truth* (2023).

About the Series

This series offers concise and structured introductions to all aspects of the philosophy of Søren Kierkegaard. Some Elements are organized around particular themes, while others are devoted to specific Kierkegaardian texts. Both well-established and emerging scholars contribute to the series, combining decades of expertise with new and different perspectives.

Cambridge Elements ☰

Philosophy of Søren Kierkegaard

Elements in the Series

Kierkegaard, Socrates, and the Meaning of Life
Rick Anthony Furtak

A full series listing is available at: www.cambridge.org/EPSK

Printed in the United States
by Baker & Taylor Publisher Services